Perfect & Peace

Lloyd John Ogilvie

HARVEST HOUSE PUBLISHERS
Eugene, Oregon 97402

Cover by Left Coast Design, Portland, Oregon

PERFECT PEACE

Copyright © 2001 by Lloyd John Ogilvie
Published by Harvest House Publishers
Eugene, Oregon 97402

Library of Congress Cataloging-in-Publication Data
Ogilvie, Lloyd John.
    Perfect peace / Lloyd John Ogilvie.
        p. cm.
    Includes bibliographical references.
    ISBN 0-7369-0545-6
    1. Peace—Religious aspects—Presbyterian Church. 2. Spiritual life—Presbyterian Church. 3. Christian life—Presbyterian authors. I. Title.

BV4647.P35 O45 2001
248.4'851—dc21   00-049854

Printed in the United States of America.

01 02 03 04 05 06 07 08 09 10 / BP-MS / 10 9 8 7 6 5 4 3 2 1

To Hester and John Caldwell—

For John, an authentic peacemaker
who recently graduated to heaven,
and for Hester, who communicates radiant peace.
"Don't know when, but I know where we'll meet again."

Contents

Peace

by Henry Van Dyke

With eager heart and will on fire
I sought to win my great desire.
"Peace shall be mine," I said, but life
Grew bitter in the endless strife.

My soul was weary, and my pride
Was wounded deep. To heaven I cried.
"God give me peace, or I must die."
The dumb stars glittered no reply.

Broken at last I bowed my head
Forgetting all myself and said:
"Whatever comes, His will be done."
And in that moment peace was won.

Chapter 1

DO YOU HAVE PERFECT PEACE?

Now may the Lord of peace
Himself give you peace always in every way.
—2 THESSALONIANS 3:16

If I were to ask, "Do you believe in God?" you would probably say, "Why yes, of course." And if I were to ask, "Do you know God?" you might respond, "Yes, and I wish I knew Him better." But if I were to ask, "Do you have a deep, consistent, abiding sense of peace?" I suspect that you would reply, "No, I don't."

It's interesting that in the Old Testament the meanings for the words *peace* and *salvation* are nearly synonymous. Yet many of us who claim that we are saved do not experience consistent peace. We don't need W. H. Auden to tell us that we live in the *Age of Anxiety*. It's all around us. The difficulty with most of us is that there's a great discrepancy between what we believe and how we feel and think. We may be sure that we're going to live forever, but we sometimes have a hard time getting through life with a daily sense of God's peace.

A Peace Inventory

I want to be very personal in asking you a few questions. Please try to respond as honestly as you can. Here are four possible responses to the questions: never, seldom, frequently, consistently.

Do you have peace of mind? Is your mind controlled by the Spirit of God? Or is your mind filled with a jumble of unresolved grievances, unfinished plans, and frustrating disappointments? Right at this moment can you say that your mind is at peace? *Never? Seldom? Frequently? Consistently?*

Are your feelings at peace? You know that feelings *do* matter. How we feel affects how we live and how we relate to others. Do you *feel* at peace right now? Are you free from smouldering anger, nagging fears, frustration, and envy? *Never? Seldom? Frequently? Consistently?*

Do you have a sense of peace about your desires? Are you clear about God's will for your life? Do you trust in His daily guidance? Are you certain about your goals? Are you free from conflict between what you want and what you sense God wants? *Never? Seldom? Frequently? Consistently?*

Since your relationships with people have so much to do with how you experience peace, do you let others rob you of inner peace? Are you at peace with others? *Never? Seldom? Frequently? Consistently?*

And what about circumstances? Do you allow circumstances to disrupt your ability to be at peace? Do you remain calm in the face of trouble? *Never? Seldom? Frequently? Consistently?*

Finally, is your body at peace? Are you strained by stress, agitation, nervousness? Or are you free from tension, churning stomach, tight muscles, high blood pressure? Do you have a sense of calmness in your body? *Never? Seldom? Frequently? Consistently?*

The Wholeness of True Peace

Note that this peace inventory includes the whole being—mind, emotions, will, body, relationships, and circumstances. That's because true peace is wholeness—mental health, emotional stability, volitional integration, and physical well-being. When this quality of peace reigns in you, it cannot be debilitated by people or circumstances.

True peace cannot be broken by life's storms. Untainted by care, untouched by the highest surges of sorrow, unstained by unforgiven sin, true peace is indefatigable and actually grows deeper with the challenges and trials of life. Do you have this kind of pervasive peace? Do I?

Why Don't We Have Perfect Peace?

I came to grips with this question one summer during a solitary retreat. As I reviewed the preceding inventory, I realized that I would have to respond either *seldom* or *frequently* to most of the questions. And I asked myself, "Why can't I answer *consistently?* Why is it that I don't know more of the peace of God if, indeed, I believe in God? I've been a Christian for more than 50 years. Why are there some days when peace eludes me?"

So many of us share a longing for lasting peace, but we are unsure of the litmus test of salvation: abiding inner peace that endures difficult people and disturbing circumstances.

This is the reason that the Lord has led me to do a prolonged, in-depth, penetrating study on the meaning of the peace of God. In the following pages I want to present an unhurried, personal communication of the meaning of true peace, the flaws in our natures that resist peace, the peace Christ revealed, the peace won through the blood of His cross, how to endure pain with peace, how to be communicators of peace to others, and how to work for peace in our society.

PRAYER FOR PERFECT PEACE

Dear God, who longs for me to receive true peace, show me what robs me of this wonderful gift. I really want to know, Father, so I can be specific in confession and commitment to change. The inventory I've just taken alarms me with my lack of peace. I ask You to help me as I read this book about Your perfect peace. May Your promises of peace in the Bible become real for me. You know how often I live with worry, anxiety, frustration, and fear. In the quiet of this honest prayer, I open myself for You to teach me the secret of lasting peace. Thank You in advance for whatever it will take to help me receive Your peace so generously offered to me. In the name of the Prince of Peace. Amen.

Chapter 2

HOW TO HAVE CONSISTENT PEACE

*You will keep him in perfect peace, whose mind is
stayed on You, because he trusts in You.
Trust in the LORD forever, for in YAH, the LORD,
is everlasting strength.*
—ISAIAH 26:3-4

My mind drifts back over the years. I picture the people gathered in my beloved congregations. I search in memory's cherished album of faces, slipping through the pages in search of anyone I can remember who experienced consistent peace.

Then a disturbing thought hits me. Why are there so few people I can recall who exude peace regardless of problems or perplexities? Why don't I know more of them now? Why is it true peace seems to be such a rare trait in people who believe in God?

A few faces come to me. They are young and old, rich and poor, highly educated and self-taught, men and women. Yet they all have this one thing in common: They are unruffled, imperturbable, unflappable, unhurried. They all have perfect peace.

Strangely enough, many of these people have suffered difficult circumstances, endured physical pain, and have routinely coped with troublesome people. And yet, each of them manifests a profound, palpable sense of peace. I have felt it when I've been with them. They are centered, at ease with themselves, and in love with the Lord. Their serenity startles me, their reliance on a silent inner strength inspires me, and their resiliency in tense times always encourages me.

What are the qualities that allow these people to experience the kind of peace that is unassailable by the surging storms of life?

How would you like to experience that kind of consistent peace? A peace that lasts in the midst of conflict? A peace that holds together when your world falls apart?

The Source

There is only one source of that kind of consistent peace—God. Throughout the Bible, language is stretched to distinguish God's true peace from temporary, transitory peace. Jesus carefully distinguished His peace from the world's peace. Paul talked about a peace that surpasses all understanding. Peter offered "multiplied peace" to early Christians in his epistle. In each case it is the same: an effort to set divine peace off and above, as something different— something that men and women cannot produce on their own. The Bible is clear: We can't make peace, but we can receive it.

God's peace is superlative—excellent, the greatest, matchless, peerless, supreme, unparalleled, unrivaled, unsurpassed.

It is so important that we understand the superlative nature of God's peace as we begin our study of authentic peace. The peace of God is His unrivaled authority. He is the creator, sustainer, and gracious redeemer of the universe. He is omniscient, knowing all from the beginning to the end; He is omnipotent, all-powerful, dependent on nothing and no one else; He is omnipresent, everywhere and yet present to those who allow Him into their lives.

There is unity of purpose in the peace of God: the oneness shared by the persons of the Godhead: Father, Son, and Holy Spirit. There is no discord or disagreement between them, only mutual glorification. And there's no panic in heaven. This is what we mean when we talk about the peace of God. For us, it means accepting the complete control of the one who is in control. There is no real peace without a firm conviction of the sovereignty of God!

Isaiah's Three Secrets

How do we fill our lives with this superlative peace, this magnificent peace of God, the peace He shares with the Son and the Holy Spirit, this peace of heaven?

The twenty-sixth chapter of Isaiah is a strategic place to begin to find the answer. It was written as a song for the people of Israel to sing both in repentance and in return to the Lord. Its implications and application for us at the beginning of the twenty-first century are unmistakable. The people of Judah, and especially of Jerusalem, had abandoned the way of faith in God for dependence on foreign powers such as Aram, for collective strength in each other, and for self-reliance. The result was neither political nor personal peace. They did not realize that security cannot be found in associative strength or sturdy self-reliance. It was not until they understood this that they could return to the Lord—the only source of peace in time of turmoil—and sing of His majesty and might, glory and goodness, providence and power.

A Mind Stayed on God

The third and fourth verses of Isaiah's song command attention not just because they are familiar but because they give us secrets to lasting peace. "You will keep him in perfect peace, whose mind is stayed on You, because he trusts in You. Trust in the LORD forever, for in YAH, the LORD, is everlasting strength."

The English words of verse 3 have been a cherished promise for God's people through the centuries. "You will keep him in perfect peace." At first we are tempted to get at the meaning of the quality of peace God offers by defining the word *perfect*. We say that *perfect peace* is "complete peace, peace that is found in tranquil surroundings and with agreeable people." But this only touches the outskirts of what Isaiah meant.

The word *perfect* is not in the Hebrew text. Rather the word for "peace," *shalom*, is repeated twice: *shalom, shalom*, like "holy, holy." Alec Motyer calls this a "super-superlative."

"This is unlike other super-superlatives in the Bible," according to my friend, Rabbi Yechiel Eckstein, the founder and president of the International Fellowship of Christians and Jews. "In this instance, the second use of the word *shalom* is not so much for emphasis as it is for definition and interpretation. For example, we might say, 'John is a fine man, fine in the sense that he is good to his children.' This can be proven by the fact that in the Hebrew text there is a vertical line between the two words of *shalom* to show precisely this idea: *shalom|shalom.*"

This idiom of duplication distinguishes pseudo-peace from God's peace, which is total peace encompassing all dimensions of the mind, emotion, will, and body as well as relationships, sense of righteousness, and perception of justice for living.

The first step to this kind of peace, according to Isaiah, is to stay our minds on God. "You will keep him in *shalom, shalom,* whose mind is stayed on You."

The Hebrew word for "mind" used here is *yēser.* It means "the constitution or tendency of the mind," what we might call a "frame of mind" or a "mind-set"—a total way of looking at things. Another way of putting it would be the "focus of our attention" or "what we have on our minds most of the time." *Yēser* corresponds closely to the Greek word *phroneite* as used in Philippians 2:5: "Let this mind be in you which is also in Christ Jesus." Precisely translated, it means, "Let this be your attitude."

J. N. Oswalt points out in his commentary on Isaiah, "As a noun *yēser* frequently refers to that which is formed, often thoughts, purposes, or intentions. As reflected in the present translation, the Hebrew seems to place 'the steadfast mind' in an emphatic position in an independent clause at the beginning of the sentence." Practically, this means that God's superlative peace is given to those whose minds are intentionally riveted on Him. As Paternus said to his son, "Bear God on your mind constantly. See Him everywhere for there is no place where He is not."

We must keep our minds stayed on God. The Hebrew word for "stayed" is *samûk.* The wonderful thing is that *samûk* is a passive participle. It's something God does. He stays our minds on Him. As we start the day, we need only say, "Lord, I belong to You. I've been called out of this world to glorify You, to experience Your love and forgiveness, and to know peace in spite of what's going on around me. Now, Lord, I ask You for what You are more ready to give than I am willing to receive. Stay me, Lord. Stay me on Yourself. Interrupt me. Stop me. Permeate my thoughts. Call me back to You. Keep me stayed on You."

And He'll do it. If your mind wanders off, then it wanders off to a place that God wants you to deal with. Don't worry about a wandering mind. Just follow the wandering, and you'll end up someplace where God wants you to deal with an issue, a relationship, a concern, a problem. Too many people complain, "I begin to pray, and my mind wanders off." I say, "Wonderful! Let it wander and then bring God with you, and if you bring Him into your wandering, you'll soon find out the thing that's keeping you from Him."

What a great assurance! You can go to work tomorrow morning knowing that God is not going to let you get Him off your mind. He's not going to let you, because you belong to Him.

And what about the rest of the day? Do you have to become a victim of people and circumstances? Definitely not! The one confidence nothing and no one can take from you is your ability to pray without ceasing. The shams of life may rage around you, but inside there will be calm because you can pray your way through it all. You can pray in the midst of uncertainties, conflict, turmoil, and adversity. Prayer will stay your mind on God and fill your thoughts with His peace. You can pray before, during, and after challenging conversations with people. You can claim peace when you are in the most alarming, disquieting situations.

You also need to allow the Spirit to stay your mind on the Father in the good things. Peace and praise go together. There's a renewed, fresh gift of peace in gratitude. Think about God's signature in the beauty of the natural world, the way God works out solutions to your needs, the wondrous gift of people He uses to help you, and the open doors of opportunity He sets before you. What a wonderful way to live!

Jesus knew this secret. He challenged His disciples—and He challenges us—to seek first the kingdom of God. I like the way the New English Version of the Bible translates this verse, Matthew 6:33: "Set your mind on God's kingdom...before everything else!"

The kingdom of God is His sovereignty in action, His reign and rule over everything. So, setting your mind on the kingdom is the same thing as staying your mind on the rule of God. There is no peace apart from seeking to know and to do God's will. His guidance is not some mysterious set of sealed orders. We can discover far more of God's will from His commandments and from Jesus' life than most people readily acknowledge. Through the guidance of the Holy Spirit, we are also given specific direction. I'm convinced that the Spirit does speak to our hearts; we are given "words of knowledge" about situations and people and we can hear them if we listen attentively. A mind stayed on God—set on the kingdom—is a mind with spiritual eyes to see and perceptive ears to hear.

A Heart Filled with Trust

This leads us to Isaiah's second secret for receiving the *shalom, shalom* superlative peace of God. First, a mind stayed on God. And second, a heart filled with trust. The parallelism "because he trusts in You" literally translates "because in You, trust is reposed." Faith, throughout the Scripture, is a gift of the Spirit. It is not produced by us; it is received as an endowment from God. It is astounding to think about God's power to engender faith. God is so desirous of imparting His peace to us that He brings forth in us what He wants from us. He produces the stayed mind and the trust so that we don't miss out on His superlative peace!

The people of Judah trusted in human leaders and not in the Lord. They lost the Lord's peace as a result. Note the confession in Isaiah 26, verses 12 to 14: "LORD, You will establish peace for us, for You have also done all our works in us. O LORD our God, masters besides You have had dominion over us; but by You only we make mention of Your name. They are dead, they will not live; they are deceased, they will not rise."

Experiencing the peace which comes from personal knowledge of God's sovereignty requires putting trust in Him, not in leaders, friends, mates, or parents. We must trust God and love people and never turn that around. Of course, if we are to love God, we must put our ultimate trust in Him only. Peace is broken when we depend on people to provide what only God can provide. "Trust in the LORD with all your heart, and lean not on your own understanding; in all your ways acknowledge Him, and He shall direct your paths" (Proverbs 3:5-6). People were never meant to be our sources of security. When we demand that they meet our needs, we make them diminutive gods; we take our stayed eyes off the Lord God and disconnect ourselves from the consistent flow of His peace.

Peace results from a disciplined life of prayer which manifests intimate fellowship with God and the assurance of adequate resources from Him. Trusting in the sovereign God means leaving the results to Him, knowing our calling is not to be successful but to be faithful. And guess what? Real success in life means living without the worry, fretting, or care that comes from trying to control everything ourselves.

Dependence on the Rock of Ages

Now we are ready for Isaiah's third secret. Look at verse 4: "Trust in the LORD forever, for in YAH, the LORD, is everlasting strength." The Hebrew meaning of *trust* here is "to lean on Him." Have you been leaning on God? I've learned to lean on Him more lately than I've ever leaned on Him in my life, and you know what? He's reliable. He'll hold you, and He'll pick you up when you stumble. When you're weak, He'll make you strong. He stays your mind on Him so that you can take those very things that would rob you of peace and say, "Lord, please help me." And He will when you lean on Him.

Then Isaiah goes on, "For He is an everlasting strength." What he really means is He is the Rock of Ages. It is from this reference that Augustus Toplady in 1776 wrote what has become one of the most famous and cherished hymns in Christian history, "Rock of Ages, cleft for me, let me hide myself in Thee."

Keeping the flow of Isaiah's thought before us, perfect peace is the gift of God to those who allow Him to stay their minds on Him, who receive the gift of trust in Him, and who depend on Him as the Rock, Foundation, and Fortress of their lives.

Our Rock's dependable, saving actions provide the fortresslike protection which we all need during menacing times. In the Old Testament, "rock" is a broad symbol for divine strength—hence our English translation: "everlasting strength."

The Prince of Peace

It's not surprising that Isaiah's thought should move from peace through trust to the foundation of that trust in God's strength and salvation. In the Scriptures, trust and faith do not exist in a vacuum. Faith is the result of the saving acts of God in the past, present, and future. Salvation is not an occasional intervention by God but an attribute of God. He is the "saving God." Isaiah looked back on the saving acts of God in his people's history, but also he looked forward with steady eyes for the coming of the Messiah, the Prince of Peace. "For unto us a Child is born, unto us a Son is given; and the government will be upon His shoulder. And His name will be called Wonderful, Counselor, Mighty God, Everlasting Father, Prince of Peace. Of the increase of His government and peace there will be no end" (Isaiah 9:6-7).

We have come full circle to the inseparable relationship between salvation and peace. The superlative peace God offers us comes from the Prince of Peace. Christ came in human flesh to reveal how this perfect peace can be lived in complete trust of the Father. Talk about an example of a mind stayed on the Father! In Christ, we see complete trust, the absolute surrender of will, the unswerving obedience that is the essence of true peace. He went to the cross to atone for our sins and reconcile us to God. Faith in His atoning death brings us forgiveness and new birth. Life begins all over again. We become new creatures. As our reigning Lord, He becomes the Peace of God with us. He has the authority to baptize and fill us daily with the Holy

Spirit. Everything necessary to provide us with perfect peace has been done. Peace comes to us as the magnificent gift of the Trinity: the Father's sovereign act of sending His Son and reconciling us through His shed blood; the risen Christ, Lord of our lives; and the Holy Spirit, the Spirit of peace indwelling us. Staying our minds on the Triune God gives us superlative peace indeed!

Why Do We Still Lack Peace?

Knowing all this, why do we still lack peace? The answer is quite simple. We focus our attention on things, people, possessions, success, and most of all, on ourselves. Peace of mind is lost, emotional turmoil sets in, a battle of wills with the sovereign Lord is engaged, and our bodies receive the brunt of the stress that hits us with full force.

In the midst of the turmoil and the frustration, if we turn our eyes to the cross, we will see the manifestation of God's love for us that we might know the transfer of the peace of heaven to our hearts. And when we accept the forgiveness of Jesus Christ and the cross, His Spirit comes to live in us and we know a peace that passes understanding—a peace that doesn't stop.

Again and again, Perfect Peace Himself comes to us and says, "Had enough? Tired and weary? Ready for *shalom, shalom?* Let Me give you the power to stay your mind on the Father; allow Me to give you trust; accept My strength. I'm the solid rock on which you can stand. Rest in Me! And now receive a fresh infilling of the Holy Spirit of peace."

Shalom, shalom to you!

PRAYER FOR CONSISTENT PEACE

Gracious Lord, I long for consistent peace, and I thank You for offering it to me. O Lord, help me to yield my heart and mind to You and rivet my attention on You. Now in this quiet moment, I yield to You the very things that cause me to lose my sense of peace. I commit them to You and ask that Your will be done. Praise be to You, Lord. Amen.

Chapter 3

THE PEACE THAT COMES FROM KNOWING GOD

Be of good comfort, be of one mind, live in peace;
and the God of love and peace will be with you.
—2 CORINTHIANS 13:11

There is nothing more important. With it, life is sublime; without it, there can be no peace. It is the secret to living without stress, the source of lasting happiness, the supply of wisdom beyond our understanding, the storehouse of strength to endure tough times, and the springboard to success in reaching what really counts. It is our ultimate goal, life's greatest privilege, and our most urgent need.

What I am talking about is the one essential ingredient for perfect peace. It should demand our constant attention and become the primary purpose and passion of our lives. It is more valuable than the people in our lives, and yet it will make us communicators of love, joy, and hope to those around us. It takes priority over any power we will ever wield, any position we'll ever achieve, or any portfolios we'll ever accumulate.

Our nation is in grave trouble because of the lack of this sublime quality. Lack of it accounts for the growth of moral and ethical relativism and the demise of absolutes in our society. The fabric of our values is torn and frayed because of neglect of this privilege offered to us. It is the reason we were born and the primary mission of our lives.

What is this valuable privilege?

Knowledge of God.

We cannot have peace until we know God. Yet, many people who desperately desire to have peace would have to admit that they really do not know God. For others, lacking knowledge of God causes vacillating spirituality, inconsistency between the talk and walk of their faith, ineffectiveness in prayer, and lack of courage for life's challenges and crises. For still others, inadequate knowledge of God accounts for vague values and equivocating ethics. And for so many, the absence of the knowledge of God causes intellectual confusion, emotional turmoil, and physical tension. This deficit results in an abject loneliness no person can relieve, emptiness no amount of material success can fill, and anxiety no therapy or drug can heal.

H. G. Wells said, "Civilization is in a race between education and catastrophe." I say we are in a race between knowledge of God and catastrophe.

The Primary Purpose of Your Life

Allow me to speak very directly and personally. I have chosen not to trifle with trivialities or platitudes. I want to reach into the very core of the need in America and the very essence of what I suspect is the most profound need in the life of everyone who reads this book. I want to go deep into the primary purpose of your life: to really know God and to grow daily in a personal relationship with Him that brings a complete sense of peace into your life and allows you to serve the world around you.

There's a reason I have chosen to write about your need to know God. It is because during the past 50 years, I've had the privilege of caring for business, professional, academic, political, and entertainment leaders. Profound, unguarded, honest conversations with them through the years have led me to take no one for granted. I have been astounded by frank admissions from highly successful, prominent, and influential leaders that they do not have an ever-deepening knowledge of God. Some have strong religious loyalties; others pray in times of need or crises; and still others are quick to affirm their belief in God and the values of the Judeo-Christian tradition. However, over the years as I've asked people, "What would you say is the real purpose or goal of your life?" very few have said, "To know God." I've heard thousands respond that their purpose was to be successful, to be a good parent, to contribute to society, or even to serve God, but seldom has knowing God been mentioned. Is that because it is too personal? I don't think so. Rather it is because so many have missed the delight of really knowing God. If we make no effort to know God, how can we expect to experience His perfect peace?

God's Desire for Us to Know Him

What the Lord said to Israel through the prophet Hosea may very well be the Lord's word for our time. In fact, it sounds like a headline in a contemporary newspaper!

> There is no truth or mercy or knowledge of God in
> the land. By swearing and lying, killing and stealing
> and committing adultery, they break all restraint....My
> people are destroyed for lack of knowledge.
>
> —HOSEA 4:1-2,6

But wait! Combine that diagnosis with a hopeful prognosis through Jeremiah, if we will receive it:

> I will put My law in their minds, and write it on their
> hearts; and I will be their God, and they shall be My
> people. No more shall every man teach his neighbor,
> and every man his brother, saying, "Know the LORD,"
> for they all shall know Me, from the least of them to
> the greatest of them, says the LORD. For I will forgive
> their iniquity, and their sin I will remember no more.
>
> —JEREMIAH 31:33-34

When God's purpose for us becomes our basic priority, we begin to experience His peace. I want you to accept both the alarming diagnosis of Hosea and the assuring prognosis in Jeremiah of God's intent to have you know Him.

What Does It Mean to Know God?

What does it mean really to know God and to live with a knowledge of Him? Knowledge of God is more than ideas about Him. It involves three of the most misunderstood and distorted words of our time. We must return to their original meanings rather than culture's misuse of them. Knowledge of

God involves *intimacy*, *integrity*, and *intentionality*. Let me illustrate what I mean.

Intimacy with God

The use of the word *intimacy* to explain the depth of the relationship God wants with us may sound presumptuous to some, preposterous to others. But let the word stand. The word *intimacy* means "proceeding from within, inward, internal." The intimacy of the *Thou-I* relationship we were created to experience with God requires the opening of our innermost thoughts to Him just as He has revealed His innermost nature to us. The Hebrew word for *knowledge* has the same root as "to know." It also means "the physical and spiritual oneness of a husband and wife." That gives us a clue to the closeness and completeness God wants with us.

"It was back in 1984 when I realized I needed to get closer to God," a senator once told me. "One of my very dear friends—someone whom I had worked with over the years—was diagnosed with cancer. It was such a gloomy period, I decided to take time out for a retreat. I went to a Jesuit retreat house to think about my life. During that quiet time, I began to think about my relationship with God. Afterwards, I enrolled in a prayer group, taking a six-month period to pray and reflect.

"In the course of that time, I began thinking about my future. I had a safe seat in the House of Representatives, and I liked what I was doing. But I was approaching 50 years of age, and I wanted something new. I didn't necessarily want a new job. I wanted a new life. The senior senator in my state was coming up for reelection. I didn't know his plans, but I knew I had to decide on mine. So I assembled the usual political advisors and good friends. I also began going through a process that in my faith we call discernment. Discernment is different from decision-making in that you really ponder what God's will is for you.

"As I began to think about God's will for me, I reached out to a Catholic nun who was known for guiding people who were in the discernment process. I selected her because she was well-grounded in a spiritual framework and involved with the Lord, and she had no stake in the outcome. You see, when you consult with political advisors, they have a stake. Consult with pollsters—they want to bring you good news. What I needed at this time was a different kind of good news!

"So, for about the next year and a half, I met weekly with my advisor for prayer, reflection, and guidance. She reviewed some of the approaches of St. Ignatius of Loyola about God's will. She encouraged me to think about it and to write about it, and we talked about it. It was like peeling an onion. As the elections drew closer, I knew that it was God's will for me to run. I just had to trust and let go. Let go of safety. Let go of security. Take a risk. Seek a higher office.

"I did not believe it was God's will that I win. I don't believe in a Ouija-Board kind of Christianity where you ask God for the answer to the secrets of the future. I'm not talking about that. I knew there was no guarantee. The only guarantee was that I would be doing God's will by running and that, even if I lost, that was part of the plan too. Winning or losing would take me to the new life that God intended for me. Of course I wanted to win, so I wasn't giving up in complete abandonment with no effort on my behalf. I did what any good candidate does. But I had the inner peace of knowing in my heart that, in January of that year, God would have me exactly where I needed to be."

Developing an ever-deepening knowledge of God demands this same kind of discernment process—one that involves the total inner being: intellect, emotion, and will. God knows all about what's going on inside us. We cannot hide from Him. When we begin to know God, to start a relationship with Him, we take the first step in acknowledging that He knows all about us, and we allow Him to meet us at the point of our anguish or anxiety, joy or pain, hurt or hope. The psalmist expressed it like this: "O LORD, You have searched me and known me" (Psalm 139:1). The psalmist yielded his inner being to God when He realized he was known by Him: "Search me, O God, and know my heart; try me, and know my anxieties; and see if there is any wicked way in me, and lead me in the way everlasting" (Psalm 139:23-24). This is the true path to inner peace.

I wondered about the inner peace the senator had experienced before the election. Had it stayed with her in the midst of her heavy responsibilities here at the Senate?

"It's like a tide," she told me. "It ebbs and flows. I have high and low tides of peace. But when you have faith, you never hit dry ground. I'm so grateful for the gift of faith. I grew up surrounded by people of faith. My faith is like a home where I can always turn to God, and I have the peace that comes from knowing I am always welcome."

Knowing God begins with the astounding assurance that, inspite of what we've done or been, His love will not change. You and I were created to be loved by God and to love Him. The love relationship is where knowledge of God begins and never ends. Today, the LORD says, "I love you; I will never let you go; you are Mine! I have chosen and called you to know Me and be known!" We experience an intimate union with God when we receive His love, accept

His forgiveness, and turn our lives over to His control. We know *who* we are when we accept *whose* we are. This is the secure source of peace. It is the core of psychological health, godly self-esteem, profound self-acceptance, and the realization that each of us is a unique, never-to-be-repeated miracle of God's creativity.

True knowledge of God is nurtured by prayer. It always starts with God. He is consistently beforehand, seeking us. Our desire to pray arises because He wants to love, guide, inspire, and empower us. And the greatest gift we can receive in prayer is more of God Himself! Whatever He gives is nothing in comparison to the peace that comes with knowing Him better. And whatever He withholds is always to draw us closer to Him.

> Thus says the LORD: "Let not the wise man glory in his wisdom, let not the mighty man glory in his might, nor let the rich man glory in his riches; but let him who glories glory in this, that he understands and knows Me, that I am the LORD, exercising lovingkindness, judgment, and righteousness in the earth. For in these I delight," says the LORD.
>
> —JEREMIAH 9:23-24

Integrity of Character

Knowledge of God also involves integrity. Here's another word that's used and misunderstood a lot these days. The word *integrity* means "undivided wholeness, unimpaired completeness." It entails congruity of behavior, consistency between what we believe and what we do. Intimacy with God, knowing Him as He has revealed Himself, must be inseparably intertwined with His character and commandments. In case you wondered, the Ten Commandments have not gone out of style. Along with Jesus' eleventh commandment that we are to love as He has loved us, the commandments provide the absolutes for living our lives in peace.

When was the last time you reviewed God's absolutes for living? We live in a time when God's absolutes are often replaced by a reckless moral and ethical relativism. Situational ethics have come home to roost. Our standards are determined by the polls, and polls reflect a culture adrift from God's absolutes. We have become advocates of antinomianism, a kind of lawlessness when it comes to God's commandments. When the prodigal son came home to his father, he didn't try to restructure his father's values to fit the far country! God's absolutes are our lifelines to peace—fixed points in a world of change.

Try this on for size. God has chosen to be our God; He has elected us to be His people. Knowing Him and receiving His peace requires integrity, the congruity of a life of faithfulness to Him. Obedience to what God reveals in our daily and moment-by-moment prayers is the secret to lasting peace. God assumes the responsibility of transforming our characters. And He knows what He's about!

We have been chosen to try out the splendor of God, to think magnificently about Him and the character transplant of peace that happens as a part of knowing Him. Everything we experience in the ups and downs of life is for what God wants to happen to us. He is the "Personsmith," hammering out our characters to be consistent with His own as revealed in Jesus Christ. Through the indwelling Spirit, we are given the fruit of the Spirit, which are really the attributes of Christ's character: not only peace, but love, joy, patience, kindness, goodness, faithfulness, meekness, and self-control. (See chapter 9 to understand how we are connected to the fruit of the Spirit.)

The more we know God, the more His character traits are manifested in us and our characters. William Penn said of George Fox, "He was an original and no man's copy." When we know God with intimacy and integrity it will be said of us, "He (or she) is Christ's copy!"

The Los Angeles Lakers' basketball coach said of Kobe Bryant, "I want him to be the next Kobe Bryant, not the next Michael Jordan." So too God wants each of us to become the unique, special person in Christ's image we were born to become.

Integrity means putting the lofty concepts of our faith to work. As e. e. cummings said, "To be nobody-but-yourself—in a world which is doing its best, night and day, to make you everybody else—means to fight the hardest battle which any human being can fight; and never stop fighting." I say to be God's person is the hardest battle, but we are not alone. What God guides, He provides!

Intentionality of Life

Intimacy and integrity result in the third dynamic ingredient of truly knowing God—intentionality. We express intentionality by setting clear goals to which we press on with courage. *Intentionality* means "acting on what we intend, what is done with intention or design—the quality or state of being intentional." Knowing God involves seeking His guidance to clarify His intent for all our relationships and responsibilities.

To know God is no safe, bland, urbane affair. Often it involves risk. The Lord constantly calls us out. He wants to get us to the place where He is our only security and assurance. Think of how hard we work to eliminate the risks of life. We work, save, plan, and invest ourselves with safe responsibilities. And yet we still lack peace. We settle into the ruts of sameness and complain that life is no longer exciting. Victor Hugo in _Les Misérables_ said, "Morality is truth in full bloom."

As long as we are alive, there will be a next step in our adventure with the Lord. He constantly calls us out from where we are to a new level of risk. There will never be a time when what we've done or who we've been can be our security. We were programmed always to be on the growing edge of new adventure. Where is the element of creative risk in your life? What would you do if you had the peace of trusting God completely? As Jim Elliot said, "He is no fool who gives what he cannot keep to gain what he cannot lose."

Baseball champion Mark McGwire was right when he said, "You never know how far you can travel until you start the trip."

Commitment to the Goal

Once we've asked the Lord to guide us in what He wants us to do we must consistently press on to do what only He could help accomplish. When the goal is clearly defined, we must commit ourselves to it. The apostle Paul knew that commitment opens the floodgates of supernatural power peace and power: "I know whom I have believed and am persuaded that He is able to keep what I have committed to Him until that Day" (2 Timothy 1:12).

It's fascinating to note that Paul goes on to remind Timothy of what had been committed to him: "That good thing which was committed to you, keep by the Holy Spirit who dwells in us" (2 Timothy 1:14).

So, there is a repeated exchange of commitment all through our lives. The Lord commits to us what He wants to do through us, and in response we commit ourselves to do what He has guided with the inflow of supernatural peace and power.

One of the most encouraging things I see happening in America today is a profound spiritual awakening among United States senators. That seldom catches the attention of the media which is so often captivated by reporting bad news. But it's happening nonetheless. And commitment seems to be the key.

In April 1998, Oklahoma Senator Jim Inhofe traveled to West Africa with a vision. He wanted to initiate in the African cabinets and parliaments small groups that would meet weekly using the Senate Prayer Breakfast group as a model.

President Mathieu Kerekou of the Republic of Benin, a Marxist dictator for 17 years, was the senator's key contact. After allowing an election, the president had been voted out of office. Then he made a new commitment to Jesus and was reelected.

Senator Inhofe visited with him at his home for more than four hours. The topic of discussion was how to use Jesus as a role model for leadership. Since that time Senator Inhofe has visited Benin several more times and has developed a close friendship with the president.

Several initiatives have come out of their friendship. The president asked the senator to meet many political leaders in the region. Out of these meetings have developed new friendships and small groups focused on Jesus. Some of these countries have now begun youth corps to introduce Jesus to the poor and young of their countries. President Kerekou hosted a reconciliation conference in Benin in December 1999. He and the senator discussed the issue of seller, buyer, and victim in the history of slavery. To the 200 African-American attendees, Senator Inhofe asked for forgiveness on behalf of his ancestors who were involved in slavery. It's exciting how rapidly this seed of reconciliation is growing from the first initiative. There is really no way to list all of the positive results that continue to grow from Senator Inhofe's vision of building relationships around Jesus of Nazareth. His efforts focused on Jesus alone are bringing wonderful fruit to the peoples of Africa.

As W. H. Murray says, "The moment one definitely commits oneself, then providence moves too. All sorts of things occur to help one that would never otherwise have occurred. A whole stream of events issues from the decision, raising in one's favor all manner of unforeseen incidents and meetings and material assistance which no one could have dreamed would come his way."

Many senators in our Bible study group have discovered the unlimited spiritual power of unreserved commitment in the awesome responsibilities committed to them by God. We have claimed the instigating intentionality of a challenge stated by Wolfgang Goethe: "What you can do or dream you can do, begin it. Boldness has genius, power, and magic in it." Begin it now!

The motto of my ministry in the Senate is: "Without God We Can't; Without Us He Won't." It is so important for our growth in the knowledge of God to get that clearly set in our minds. When you know God, you can rest in peace knowing that He will guide you to the exact place where He wants you to be. You may think your choice of a vocation, where you work, whom you marry, where you live is your choice. Not so! The Lord directs you, creating in you the desire to do what He has planned for you, directing you to greatness!

Do You Know God?

Finally, that personal question I asked earlier. Do you know God? Is that relationship with Him distinguished by intimacy of prayer, integrity of life, and intentionality of commitment? Without God you can't; without you, He won't. Belong to God; become a wonder to yourself, a joy to your friends, and a servant-leader in your world, and begin to experience perfect peace!

PRAYER FOR KNOWLEDGE OF GOD

Dear Father, it is my greatest desire today to know You better. I want to have a relationship with You that is distinguished by intimacy of prayer, integrity of life, and intentionality of commitment. You have searched me, and You know me. If there is any sin in me, forgive it and lead me to the truth of Your absolutes for living. Thank You for guiding all my relationships and responsibilities. Lead my steps today so that I may live out Your intentions for my life. Give me the peace of knowing and trusting You completely. In the grace of Your beloved Son. Amen.

Chapter 4

THE ABUNDANT PEACE
OF GOD'S AMAZING GRACE

Grace to you and peace be multiplied.
—1 PETER 1:2

I sat in the bleachers at the tattoo in the Edinburgh Castle. My blood was stirred by the pipes and drums, the marching bands, and the beautiful pageantry. As part of the evening's program, groups of people from all over the world were introduced. Then we were all invited to sing "Amazing Grace" in our own native language. It was a delight to hear my favorite hymn sung in German, Japanese, and French— all blending in with the hearty voices of the Scots who sang loudest of all.

A Highland Scots friend seated next to me tugged on my arm and exclaimed, "'Tis amazin', isn't it?" Thinking he meant the grace about which we were singing, I heartily agreed and began to talk enthusiastically about what grace meant to me and the peace I experienced as a result.

My friend interrupted my discourse, "Auch, that's not what I mean. What's amazin' is that everyone knows the song and is singing it in ther' own language."

I had to agree. That in itself was amazing, but for me the grace about which we were singing was and is the most amazing of all. People all over the world know the hymn "Amazing Grace," especially the first verse, but many sing it without really understanding what it means.

At the end of the tattoo that evening, a lone piper mounted the ramparts of the castle. All the lights were turned off except one spotlight that focused on him. He played the winsome, impelling melody of "Amazing Grace" once again. The international crowd listened with rapt attention and almost breathless silence.

As the piper played with impeccable perfection, my mind's eye re-created the vision of a 22-year-old seaman and the metamorphic moment in his life that motivated the writing of "Amazing Grace." While the lone piper played on I pictured the dramatic circumstances. Remembering them always renews my experience of grace and, as a result, fresh peace.

The Raging Storm

It was March 10, 1748. For 27 days, a little three-masted ship named the *Greyhound* had been battling the tumultuous, angry sea and gale-force winds. Then on that March day, the pent-up fury of a North Atlantic gale hit with full impact. The *Greyhound's* sails were ripped to pieces, the rigging torn asunder, and the bulwarks stove in.

A young seaman was called from below to man the hand pump. Five men assigned to that duty before him had been swept into the sea. The seaman pumped desperately, trying to keep the ship from going down. It seemed like an impossible task, and the rest of the crew prepared to abandon the ship as they all hovered between life and death. The port side began to cave in. The decks were awash, and then one of the masts snapped.

As the seaman continued to pump, his short life flashed before him. He remembered his mother's death when he was seven. His sea-captain father could not leave the ship to raise him so the boy was placed in a school which he left when he turned 11 to go to sea as a deckhand. The life on board slave ships hardened him. Early in his teens he became known for his licentious lifestyle and his blasphemous tongue. On the slave ships which he sailed, he was brutal and cruel to the slaves. His life was filled with callous inhumanity and debauchery. He became a militant atheist.

Then his life went from bad to worse. Through sickness and the double-dealings of the slave trader for whom he worked collecting slaves, he was thrown into a slave compound in Sierra Leone. He was treated like one of the slaves. Chains were placed on his feet, and he was given no food.

Unexpected Kindness

If it had not been for the kindness of the slaves who had felt the snap of his whip only days before, he would have died. They saw his plight and took pity on him, sharing their meager rations with the very man who had stood over them with his cruel whip. They nursed him back to health and eventually smuggled a letter to his father aboard a passing ship. Finally, the letter reached his father in England. His father acted promptly, asking fellow sea captains headed for the African coast to look for his son and bring him home. At long last the captain of the *Greyhound* found him and took him on board. The ship was not a slaver but took on a cargo of African camwood, a buoyant wood.

The hardened, grim-beyond-his-age seaman signed on board for the long, circuitous journey to Liverpool by way of Brazil and up the coast of North America to Newfoundland where the ship would begin its crossing of the North Atlantic.

Lord, Have Mercy!

During the long, boring months, the seaman found a copy of an English translation of *The Imitation of Christ* by the Dutch monk Thomas à Kempis, and read it.

Now as the blasting winds of the gale beat upon him and the waves licked the deck of the *Greyhound*, the magnificent words of à Kempis gripped his mind. There were perhaps only minutes before he would meet the judgment of the God he had so vehemently denied. He was filled with fear, more of meeting God than the sea or death itself. The truth of his condition struck him with full force. How lost he'd been! How blind!

Suddenly the young man shouted out something that made the rest of the crew stop and stare. This ingrate youth, infamous for his lewd behavior and his foul tongue, shouted out, "Lord, have mercy!" It was so unexpected, so uncharacteristic that even the hard, bitter sailors were stunned. It was shocking to them that an atheist like this would turn to God seemingly at the last moment of his life and ask for His mercy.

His prayer was answered. Suddenly the angry sea subsided, and the *Greyhound* was stabilized. The sails and rigging were repaired, and the battered ship pressed on. When miraculously the *Greyhound* made landfall, limping into a cove near Londonderry in North Ireland on April 8, the seaman staggered off the ship and made his way to a church to pray.

Amazing Grace

The seaman's name was John Newton. Later when he became a clergyman in the Church of England, he wrote and published a book of hymns. The most memorable of them was "Amazing Grace." The tune for the hymn, surprisingly enough, came from the plantations of Virginia. It was entitled "Loving Lambs." It had been handed down by generations of slaves, some of whom Newton himself had captured and taken to America.

The hymn was published with this folk tune in 1831, 24 years after Newton's death. Since that time, it has found its way into hymnbooks of every denomination and into the hearts of people throughout the world. The tune is haunting, but the words nourish a hunger in the soul.

A profound peace settled over me when the lone piper had finished that evening in the tattoo and a full pipe and drum band picked up the melody. I was brought back to the present by a nudge from my Scots friend. He said, "I've been thinking about what you said about God's grace and peace. 'Tis amazin', isn't it!"

Amazing indeed! Secular and spiritual people join together in singing this remarkable confession of need and resounding confidence in grace—the essential aspect of God's nature. How could God's perfect peace be avoided in this setting?

Do You Ever Feel Wretched or Lost?

Consider the words "That saved a wretch like me! I once was lost, but now am found, Was blind, but now I see." I have a friend who is a popular singer. He always changes the word *wretch* to *soul*. He argues that people don't feel wretched today. But what about the epidemic proportions of anxiety and lack of peace in people's hearts today? I devote all of chapter 7 to that subject.

And what about feeling lost? We pretend we know exactly where we are and where we are going. Our fast-moving lives heading toward what looks like clearly defined goals make the words "I once was lost" sound irrelevant.

But haven't you ever felt lost? Maybe you feel lost right now. Certainly, we've all had times of loneliness. And who hasn't had a feeling of being estranged or out of touch with God?

Look at it this way. If our ultimate purpose is to know God and enjoy Him, then anything less than an intimate relationship with Him means we're lost. We can get lost in the asphalt jungle, in a life crowded with people, success, business, and prosperity. Our lostness may stem from a combination of pride and self-sufficiency that keeps us from prayer. Or we can get lost in religion, worshiping the idols of our denomination, or in church activities. But no matter how lost we are, God's grace and peace are always there for us. We just need to receive them!

God's Gift of Grace

Grace is God's gift to us. It is a confirmation of His unqualified love for us. Some people think they only need grace at the beginning of the Christian life. That's not true. We could not live a day without a fresh supply of grace. Sadly, however, some of us try. And then we realize we also lack peace. And we wonder why.

Is there any place in your life where you are saying, "No!" to God's grace? Authentic grace will always confront anything that keeps you from an honest, open relationship with God and His peace. Here's how to recognize God's authentic grace: God will give you the gift of His grace before you even ask; He will approach you when you can't come to Him; He will give you grace that is inexhaustible out of His fullness; He will give you exactly what you need. God's grace is as predictable as the sunrise and as plentiful as the ocean. Your job is simply to receive it!

God Chooses to Give Us Grace Before We Ask

I've never met a dynamic Christian who said he or she found Christ, got His attention, and then began a relationship with Him. Rather, they say, "He found me! And even my longing to know Him, He birthed in my heart!" He uses everything that happens to us and around us to bring us to Him. Then Christ whispers, "You are loved!"

God's grace is preexisting—that is "coming before." When used with grace, it means "beforehand love, acceptance that is given before we ask for it, forgiveness offered before we seek it, God's choice of us before we choose to be chosen." This is grace. Paul caught its dynamic quality in

Romans 5:8: "God demonstrates His own love toward us, in that while we were still sinners, Christ died for us." This too is grace.

God Comes to Us When We Can't Come to Him

Just as Christ graciously created the desire to know Him, He constantly seeks to initiate a deeper relationship with us. He has to be the one to do it. Often, when life becomes pressured, filled with problems and frustrations, we try harder to make things work out. This strategy won't work. When we get burdened down with our failures and sins, we put off seeking forgiveness. We try to be different or better to atone for what we've done or said. Because it's hard for us to admit our difficulties with people, we shift the blame to them or simply cut them out of our lives. But no matter how we sin, Christ is there for us.

The very nature of sin is that it dulls our desire to seek forgiveness and a right relationship with God. He comes to us when we can't come to Him because of self-justification and guilt. The cross stands as a constant reminder that God will not give up on us.

It's when we neglect His grace that Christ magnificently fulfills one of Isaiah's messianic prophecies, which, by the way, follows the promise of enjoying life. "And My elect shall long enjoy the work of their hands.... It shall come to pass that before they call, I will answer; and while they are still speaking, I will hear" (Isaiah 65:22,24).

Christ also motivates us in the desire to pray! He invades our minds with the realization of our needs, guides us to the wording of our prayers, and intercedes on our behalf to the Father. When we are at last able to admit our needs, confess our sins, or seek help with problems, He breaks our bonds, frees us to cry out for help, and sends us peace.

God Gives Us His Fullness

The grace Christ mediates to us is indefatigable. Consider the amount of grace you receive each day as a matter of course: grace that He found you; grace that He filled you with His Spirit; grace that intervenes in hundreds of serendipities each day; grace to cry out for Him when you are down; grace to praise Him when you count your blessings; grace when you are ill; grace when you need wisdom and love for people; grace to see you through trials; grace to die victoriously; grace to live forever; grace heaped upon grace to fill you with His perfect peace.

I like the way John puts it in his Gospel: "And the Word became flesh and dwelt among us, and we beheld His glory, the glory as of the only begotten of the Father, full of grace and truth. And of His fullness we have all received, and grace for grace" (John 1:14,16).

We simply cannot diminish God's supply of grace. Receiving grace is like draining water from the Atlantic Ocean with a teaspoon. The supply of grace exceeds the waters of all the seas.

God Knows Exactly What You Need

God's supply of grace is also fitting. In a time of physical need, Christ's assurance to Paul was, "My grace is sufficient for you…" (2 Corinthians 12:9). The word _sufficient_ here not only means "adequate" but also "fitting." The grace Christ provides is fit for your needs, perfectly matched for what you are going through in the ups and downs of life. Looking back on what you've faced, how many times could you have said,

"The Lord knew exactly what I needed?" This gives us a confident hope for the future. Fitting grace, grace that is suited to our specific needs, the grace of Jesus Christ always brings peace.

Receiving My
Gift of Grace

I still remember the freshness and freedom I felt the first time I truly experienced the peace that comes with healing grace. I was a postgraduate student at the University of Edinburgh. Because of financial pressures, I had to carry a double load of classes that were very demanding. I was exhausted by the constant feeling of never quite measuring up. No matter how good my grades were, I thought they could be better. Sadly, I was not living the very truths I was studying. Although I could have told you that the Greek words for *grace* and *joy* are *charis* and *chara*, I was not experiencing them.

One day in the corridor of New College, my beloved professor, Dr. James Stewart, stopped me. He looked into my eyes and then into my soul. Then he smiled warmly, took my coat lapels into his hands, drew me down to a few inches from his face and said, "Dear boy, you are loved now!"

That night was a triumphant transition for me into the state of God's liberating grace—love that's given before we either deserve it or ask for it. I think of Dr. Stewart's words every day and on some days every hour. "Jesus Christ is the same yesterday, today, and forever" (Hebrews 13:8). He is God's grace with us.

Through the years I've enjoyed sharing my story with people who need grace. I usually explain how Grace Himself, the Lord Jesus, works in their hearts. Together we review the salient passages of Scripture about grace.

Then I ask them: "Do you want to receive it?" I've never had a person say, "No!"

After we get on our knees and accept the gift of grace, I lead them in repeating a prayer so they can give as much as they know of themselves to as much as they know of Christ.

The Grace of the Father's Heart

Have you ever really stopped to think about Jesus Christ? Let your mind soar. Think magnificently about the Christ. Catch the magnitude and majesty of His life with the Father who, "according to His own purpose and _grace_ which was given to us in Christ Jesus before time began...has now been revealed by the appearing of our Savior Jesus Christ, who has abolished death and brought life and immortality to light through the gospel " (2 Timothy 1:9-10, emphasis added).

Christ _is_ the grace of the Father's heart. The writers of the New Testament affirm the grace of the Lord Jesus. It was grace incarnate that dwelt in Jesus of Nazareth. "Grace and truth came through Jesus Christ" (John 1:17). And what He revealed about the giving, forgiving love of grace in His message, His ministry, and His relationships gives us a liberating look into the gracious heart of God.

Peace Happens

Peace is what happens when we accept the grace of Christ. The battle within us is over. Estrangement from the

Lord is past. Peace is forgiveness. Peace is trusting. Peace is giving our worries over to Christ and leaving the results to Him. Peace is *equipoise*—the equal balance of our needs with the inflow of Christ's love, wisdom, and strength. We can hear the Lord whisper, "You are loved now. Peace be in you."

Want to receive that kind of grace? It's there for you. You can be sure you have it if a profound peace settles in your inner being. Then you too can say, "'Tis amazin', isn't it!"

PRAYER FOR AMAZING GRACE

Gracious Lord, have mercy on me! Thank You for giving me the peace of knowing that when I feel lost and forsaken, You will save me with daily experiences of Your amazing grace. When I cry out to You, You will answer. Thank You for Your inexhaustible and all-sufficient grace, offered to me even before I know I need it. In the name of Jesus Christ, the grace of Your heart. Amen.

Chapter 5

THE PEACE OF A FORGIVING AND FORGIVEN HEART

For they have healed the hurt of the daughter of My people slightly, saying, "Peace, peace!" when there is no peace.
—JEREMIAH 8:11

What would you say is the opposite of peace? Turmoil? Frustration? Anxiety? Tension? Pressure?

Conditioned by our contemporary world, we use all sorts of euphemisms for something much deeper. I want you to keep your mind and heart open when I tell you what I think is the antithesis of peace. I'm told that the sure way to get people to turn you off is to mention this subject. I've seen it myself. People's faces take on a kind of dull, wide-awake stare when you broach this topic. They check out, and their minds go elsewhere. The subject of this great turnoff is sin.

The antithesis of peace is sin—unconfessed, unrepented, unforgiven sin.

Sin is a profound malignancy. Sin crouches at the door and robs us of peace. The terrible thing about sin is that it

49

deceives us about its own existence. We sin, and then we become comfortable with having sinned. Soon we're comfortable with the memory that we sinned, and after a while it's as if sin didn't even exist at all.

Static in Your Soul

Have you ever felt a little static inside your soul that robs you of peace? That static begins when you realize that you have broken one of the basic commandments, especially Jesus' commandment of love. Have you ever felt that terrible turmoil of knowing that you've hurt another person or committed verbal assassination through criticism or gossip? You won't feel comfortable with God until you get it straightened out.

A conscience is like a square peg driven into the soul. You can try and twist it until it makes a round hole and you don't feel it anymore, but it's still there.

A little boy in the midst of a spelling bee had studied all of the words carefully. He came to the words *conscience* and *conscious*. The teacher asked him if he knew the difference, and he said, "Yeah, I'm conscious of what's happening, and when I have conscience I wish it didn't happen."

Deep down inside all of us there are disturbing memories of what we've done to contradict the commandments of God. It's a wonderful thing, as Thomas Merton says, that our souls have a face called "conscience." And isn't it wonderful that we have this inbuilt chaplain of our souls who reminds us of what's right and what's wrong? Call it the conscience or the superego, it matters little as long as you know that inside of each of us there is that little monitoring device that declares to us what's right and what's wrong.

From the time we begin our training as children, we accumulate rules and regulations—what is right and what is wrong—but we also collect the mores and the dictates of our society. Very often our consciences are loaded down with so many things that we assume them all to be of equal importance with the very commandments of God.

All of us have things that we've said and done that we've never confessed to our Lord, things we've never admitted to a fellow believer, things for which we've never received healing. If there is anything on your conscience that is contrary to what God has called you to do, you will have no peace. He will not allow you to be in peace until your conscience is under the dictates of His word. And as you reach out and search for peace in your life, all of your daily activities will be an effort to hide the pain beneath the surface.

Healing from Sin

The tragedy of our time is that we have been given many nostrums for sin but not much healing. Churches sometimes offer a kind of cheap grace that doesn't offer people an opportunity to process their feelings. They never get a chance to say, "This is where I've failed, and this is where I've sinned. Now I need to confess it and repent of it and know that I am forgiven."

We are so quick to leap into the breach to tell people, "God loves you. He forgives you. He is gracious. He is kind" that people are sent away before they even have an opportunity to say, "God, forgive me."

Karl Menninger, the U.S. psychiatrist who cofounded the Menninger Clinic, may have exaggerated a bit when he said that 75 percent of the people in his hospital could be dismissed if they would face their sins, receive forgiveness, and be willing to give forgiveness. Does that sound like overstatement? It doesn't when you consider this: The beginning of healing starts with the recognition of whatever separates us from God, and whatever separates us from God is sin.

The Balm of Repentance

God saw this lack of peace in His own people, a pretentiously pious and religious lot who were short on repentance and confession in their lives. He described them using this disturbing image: "They have also healed the hurt of My people slightly, saying, 'Peace, peace!' when there is no peace.... They were not at all ashamed; nor did they know how to blush" (Jeremiah 6:14-15).

God anguished over Judah, His beloved people. Apostasy and idolatry were causing terrible things to happen. The temple had been desecrated, and there were no longer any signs of loving-kindness, judgment, or righteousness among the people.

The basic problem was that the people were not listening to God's voice. They were not being faithful and obedient to their holy God who had given them clear, unconfused commandments as to how He wanted them to live.

Jeremiah thought about the wonderful balm from the trees in Gilead. He knew that this balm had been shipped all over the world for the healing of wounds. So he asked, "Is there no balm in Gilead?" Of course there was, and he knew it. But why wasn't it being used? The balm of forgiving love that God wanted to give needed the repentance of His people to be activated. Without repentance, they remained a "slightly healed" people with a slender grace.

The Dual Nature of Grace

In the last chapter we learned about God's authentic grace. But there are two sides to grace, or it isn't God's quality grace. Stay with me here. This is so important to understand if you really want to experience the peace that comes with a forgiving and forgiven heart. Grace is both an exposure of anything that separates us from God and an exoneration that motivates confession and forgiveness. God relentlessly holds us to His judgment of our sins, and He persistently helps us receive His forgiveness.

All too often, in our way of thinking, judgment and forgiveness are separated. But in God's heart they are two sides of the same reality: His grace. He wanted to be able to both judge sin and justify sinners. Judgment and justification are inseparable to God. Justification means the complete and unconditional exoneration of the sinner. The only way for God to accomplish this is to provide a just recompense for sin and an effective reconciliation for sinners.

God sent the Messiah to be the Lamb of God, the sacrifice for the sins of the world—our sins. Through Christ, the Father became both the Just and the Justifier.

In Romans 3:23-26, we can see Calvary focused:

> For all have sinned and fall short of the glory of God, being justified freely by His *grace* through the redemption that is in Christ Jesus, whom God set forth as a propitiation by His blood, through faith, to

demonstrate His *righteousness*, because in His for-
bearance God had passed over the sins that were pre-
viously committed, to demonstrate at the present time
His righteousness, that He might be *just* and the *justifier* of the one who has *faith* in Jesus (emphasis
added).

Note the progression: righteousness, the just, the justifier, and faith. Righteousness is essentially the quality of
being right. God's righteousness is the consistent expression
of His nature. As the author of truth, He is truthful; as the
source of love, He is unchangeably faithful. God *is* love and
cannot deny His loving-kindness. However, He must judge
and condemn any and all distortions of His plan and purpose for humankind set forth in the Ten Commandments.

Added to the breaking of the commandments are the sins
of rejecting God's guidance, living on our own cleverness,
taking pride in running our own lives, causing pain and
anguish, and saying or doing brutal things to others. Add to
this the denigration of our calling to preserve the created
world in which God has written His signature.

God cannot contradict His righteous judgment and wink
at our rebellion. God's justice makes it impossible for Him
to say, "Don't worry, it doesn't matter." Think of the moral
chaos we would have if God stepped back from judgment.

God's Unlimited Love for Us

So how can God reconcile our sins without condoning
sin? How can He remain just and still be the justifier?

Out of unlimited love, our righteous God makes us right
with Him by both demanding atonement and providing it.

That's grace. Because of the sacrifice of Christ on Calvary, the Father is able to remain just and still be the justifier.

Through Calvary, sin was judged and paid for. Christ is our justification. And because of the cross and the shedding of Christ's blood, we have the peace of knowing we *are* forgiven. Two biblical words, one in Hebrew and the other in Greek, are used to describe this amazing grace of God. In Hebrew, *hesed* comes closest to the reality. It is the indefatigable loving-kindness of God who cannot give up His people to deserved punishment and final condemnation. In Greek, it is *charis*, unqualified favor, unlimited love, and unfettered acceptance. We are "justified freely by His grace through the redemption that is in Christ Jesus" (Romans 3:24). That's our source of forgiveness and lasting peace.

The cross did not change the heart of God toward us; it exposed His justice and mercy. Whatever words we use to try to explain our theory of atonement, what really happened during those six hours on Golgotha, we will hit wide of the biblical mark unless we grapple with the cross as both the sacrifice for sin and the forgiveness and acceptance of the sinner.

Beginning with Adam, the tale of human history is a long saga of rebellion, resistance, and recalcitrance. Yet God persisted amazingly in giving His blessings and love. He called Israel to be His chosen people and gave them His blessing. Throughout the Old Testament, we see God wooing His people with love, yearning over them, intervening for their deliverance, and providing for their needs. In each period of history, we hear the loving heart of the Father calling out to His children. We hear His voice in the prophets who announced the grace of both judgment and mercy. Through Hosea's prophecy, we feel the pathos of God: "How can I give you up, Ephraim? How can I hand you over, Israel?...My heart churns within Me" (Hosea 11:8).

The prophets predicted a time when God would send His Messiah, His own Son. Those who listened to the prophets heard what Immanuel would come to do. He would become the Lamb of God for a cosmic atonement for sin. In His holiness and love, God did not wink at sin. He did not compromise either His justice or His mercy. He came in Christ to pay the full price. The cross is the once, never-to-be-repeated atonement for sinners.

There is no limit to what God will do to maintain His righteousness and justice in confronting sin and no limit to what He will do to provide forgiveness and reconciliation. That's amazing grace and abundant peace!

The Cross Through God's Eyes

There is a famous painting that depicts the meeting between John the Baptist and Jesus at the river Jordan. Jesus appears as John is speaking to the crowd. As John catches sight of Jesus, he points to Him. The artist painted John's pointing finger elongated and swollen. It seems to shout John's words, "Behold! The Lamb of God who takes away the sin of the world!" (John 1:29).

There was a cross in the heart of God before there was a cross on Calvary; the eternal heart of God was revealed on that treacherous Friday afternoon outside of Jerusalem. The cross was love and forgiveness to the utmost. As the Lamb of God was nailed on the cross, we could behold the glory of God, His manifestation of grace in time, on time, for all time.

Seeing the cross through God's eyes focuses it as His will, not an afterthought, a happenstance, or the result of a confluence of circumstances. Calvary was the result of "the determined purpose and foreknowledge of God" (Acts 2:23). The word for *counsel* in the Greek text comes from the word *bulēma*, not *thelēma*. *Thelēma* means the desire of God which, to be fully appropriated, requires our cooperation. *Boulēma* is the immutable, irrevocable will of God. He exercised His *boulēma* will when He came in Jesus Christ to reconcile the world to Himself. God couldn't be stopped. He accomplished His benevolent purpose out of sheer will. The Messiah went to the cross by the irrevocable will of God. On Calvary, God exonerated us. He set us free from guilt and condemnation and gave us perfect peace.

Winning the Battle with Death

It is so important that we understand who suffered and died on that center cross on Golgotha. What happened there is crucial for our understanding of forgiveness now and for eternity.

Did you ever wonder what Jesus thought about as He headed toward Jerusalem knowing that the cross awaited Him? He displayed awesome courage because He knew who He was and why He had come. Firmly woven in the fabric of His divine-human nature was the clear conviction that He had been born to die. His mind was steeped in the prophets, His self-identity was clearly messianic, and He knew He had been sent to do cosmic battle with sin, death, and Satan.

Look at His mission statement in Mark 10:45: "For even the Son of Man did not come to be served, but to serve, and to give His life a ransom for many." His determination to go to the cross was not an evolving decision. It didn't develop in His mind. He had read Isaiah 53 and Psalms 22 and 69. Christ did not submit to a martyr's death in order to have the memory of His gallantry forever creased into the minds of His followers. Jesus went to the cross as the atonement for our sins.

And yet it is vital to stress that Christ did not go as a helpless victim. He was fearless in telling His disciples what was going to happen because of His confidence that the Father would have the final word. Peter confessed Jesus as the Christ at Caesarea Philippi. "From that time," according to Matthew's Gospel, "Jesus began to show to His disciples that He must go to Jerusalem, and suffer many things from the elders and chief priests and scribes, and be killed, and be raised the third day" (Matthew 16:21). His death and the assurance of resurrection were inseparable in what He knew would be the mightiest of the mighty acts of God.

On the night before the crucifixion, Jesus expressed His confidence. "In the world you will have tribulation; but be of good cheer, I have overcome the world" (John 16:33).

Christ went to the cross willingly, knowing that His atoning death would bring about the reconciliation of the world. The Greek word for *reconciliation* is *apokatallassō* — a compound of *apo*, "from" and *katallassō*, "reconcile"—"to bring back to complete harmony and love." Now God's attitude toward you and me is as if we had never sinned. Through the sacrifice of Calvary we stand before God as if we had never turned away from Him or rebelled. The awesome grace! Whenever we claim the forgiveness of the cross, we are put in communion with God and He relates to us as if there had never been a transgression! Now that's amazing grace, complete healing, and perfect peace!

Healing the Malignancy

Wouldn't it be a tragedy if you went to a fine physician who took X rays of your whole body and discovered a terrible malignancy? When you came into the examining room, he ignored the malignancy and said, "Oh, well, I have a few aspirins to give you, and everything will be fine." And then he let you die.

God so loves you that He does not ignore the malignancy. "The people are saying, 'Peace, peace,' and there is no peace." There can be no peace without repentance and forgiveness and a new beginning. Can't you feel the heart of God reaching out to you from Jeremiah's prophecy?

Consider the illustration of the potter. A potter doesn't discard the distorted pots that he makes. If the pot is still wet and can be shaped, the potter keeps it on the wheel until he or she can make something out of it. The Lord taught Jeremiah that His people are like that. Even in the midst of their long exile and judgment, God said to them:

> For I know the thoughts that I think toward you, says the LORD, thoughts of peace and not of evil, to give you a future and a hope. Then you will call upon Me and go and pray to Me, and I will listen to you. And you will seek Me and find Me, when you search for Me with all your heart.
>
> —JEREMIAH 29:11-13

Accepting and
Giving Forgiveness

God sent Jesus to live among us and to declare His forgiveness. Isn't it powerful that He linked this forgiveness inseparably to our own ability to forgive others? Our wounds are healed only slightly insofar as we refuse to accept forgiveness for ourselves and give it to others.

Jesus was so concerned about our receiving and giving forgiveness as a part of the experience of peace that the only aspect of His disciples' prayer that He found necessary to exposit was the section on forgiveness: "But if you do not forgive men their trespasses, neither will your Father forgive your trespasses" (Matthew 6:15). It's only as we give forgiveness that we can appropriate it for ourselves. Yet we still hold people at arm's length, refusing to forgive them. As a result, we live in a constant state of unrest with the jarring static of unforgiveness.

How much do you really want peace? Be sure of this: You'll never know the peace of God as long as there is unforgiveness in your heart or anything in your life which contradicts the commandments of God, His revealed will in Scripture, or the words He has said to you in the depth of your own heart. The longer I live, the more sensitive I am to God's voice, and the more I'm challenged when I don't follow His direction.

The closer you come to God, the more sensitized you will become to your need to receive and give forgiveness. I am not suggesting you begin a quest for sinless perfection. I remember a man who came to a conference once. He was very angry with me. He wanted me to preach that once people truly believe in God, they will never sin again. He went on to live a very difficult life, filled with tragedy. The wound inside of him was healed only slightly because he refused to receive the forgiveness that God wanted to give him on a daily basis.

There is a direct proportion between our acceptance of forgiveness and our capacity to forgive. Christ in us assures us that we are forgiven and gives us the power to forgive. He advises us to "put on tender mercies, kindness, humility, meekness, long suffering; bearing with one another, and forgiving one another, if anyone has a complaint against another; even as Christ forgave you, so you also must do" (Colossians 3:12-13).

Forgiveness Jesus Style

If Jesus is to serve as our model and motivation, we need to remember three things about His forgiveness:

First, it is given before we sin and before we ask to be forgiven; it is His consistent and persistent disposition toward us.

Second, the Lord's forgiveness is specific. He suffered on the cross for us. Our confessions of particular needs for forgiveness receive the same grace. Each time we seek forgiveness, it is offered freely but with specific supplication. We know that we are forgiven for each sin.

Third, the forgiveness of God is realized as a result of His overtures to us. He breaks the barrier and comes to us.

That's the way God wants to forgive through us. He wants to make us people who are known for forgiveness and to have others realize that we will offer them forgiveness before they even ask. The person of Christ in us can make forgiveness an undeniable part of our personalities. People need to be assured of forgiveness, and we must take the first step in reconciliation.

That's a big order! Who can live that way? Like Peter, we want to know the limits of forgiveness: "Lord, how often shall my brother sin against me, and I forgive him? Up to seven times?" The Lord's answer is disturbing: "I do not say to you, up to seven times, but up to seventy times seven" (Matthew 18:21,22). The Hebraism *seventy-seven* is also translated "seventy times seven," meaning "without limit."

Jesus' challenge shows us that there is never a point at which we can say, "I've gone far enough! I have fulfilled the requirement. I will forgive no more."

Peter did not understand that until after the cross. It was only then that he could comprehend the secret of the Master's words: "But to whom little is forgiven, the same loves little" (Luke 7:47). The implied truth is that those who are loved deeply forgive freely. And that's exactly what God does in us. He loves and forgives. That gives us the power to become forgiving people.

Paul's Need
for Forgiveness

Paul knew all about forgiveness from his own experience. He called himself the chief of sinners. He could never dismiss the thought that Christ had loved and forgiven him in spite of all that he had done. His whole life was fired by the energy of that dominant conviction.

When he challenged the Colossians to be forgiving, he used a word that was a form of the word *grace*. The Greek word for *grace*, *charis*, is in the root of *charizomai*, "forgiveness." That kind of grace was to be expressed for all the grievances the Colossian Christians had against each other and those beyond their fellowship. The depth of the Lord's forgiveness was the inescapable standard. That little word *as* looms up in the sentence: "Forgive *as* the Lord forgave you." It means "according to, just as much as, in direct proportion, to the full degree."

Why Is Forgiving So Difficult?

That presses us to wonder: Is forgiving so difficult because we don't feel forgiven? If we are having problems forgiving, perhaps the thing we need to admit to our Lord is that we desperately need His love. Once that is real again, forgiveness will flow naturally.

I believe that Peter was right when he said, "The time has come for judgment to begin in the household of God," and that judgment begins with the discrepancies between what we believe and what we do. There is one *forgiveness* that we talk about and another *forgiveness* that we appropriate and communicate to others. We become a slightly healed people by a slender grace.

Think about those things that are crippling your peace: injustice, lack of righteousness, broken relationships. How long can you use *peace* as a mantra, saying, "peace, peace!" when there is no peace?

What about the unforgiven people in your life who are suffering simply because you have never given them the love that the Lord has given to you? True, you can't force people to repent, but you can create an atmosphere in which repentance can take place. The look on your face, the expression of your life, the way you become an initiative lover of people can create an atmosphere in which people can say, "Will you please forgive me?" To withhold forgiveness at that moment is to put your own forgiveness into jeopardy.

The great evangelist John Wesley once heard a man say, "I never forgive." His response was incisive: "Then I hope, sir, that you never sin." Indeed. Our forgiveness from God is intertwined inseparably with our willingness to forgive. The principle is so crucial that Jesus made it a central tenet of the disciples' prayer: "And forgive us our debts, as we forgive our debtors" (Matthew 6:12).

The Sad Story of Bates and Drummond

I read a story in a British magazine that shocked me. I can repeat it now because both men are dead, but to protect the innocent I will shift their names just a little bit. Bates and Drummond met at Winchester School. It was in the early 1930s. Drummond was two years ahead of Bates and, for some reason, he decided to persecute Bates miserably, persistently, and consistently for the last two years that he was at Winchester. Everything he could do to hurt him physically, to malign him publicly, to criticize him, to trick him, to hurt him, he did. Bates took it all.

Finally, Drummond graduated, and Bates finished. It was the time of the beginning of the Second World War. Bates went on to Cambridge and graduated with high honors. Drummond was not admitted to further schooling. Bates received the Distinguished Order of the British Empire for his heroic service in the British regiment. Bates went on to join the British Foreign Service and became a famous diplomat. You would know his name if I mentioned it.

Drummond had a very insignificant life. He continued to do to people—his wife, his children, people with whom he worked—what he had done to Bates. And then, just a few years ago, as Bates was seated at his prominent desk in the diplomatic office going through his mail, he found a telegram at the bottom of the pile. This is what it said: "The doctors have told me I have terminal cancer. I have two weeks to live. I cannot die without knowing that you forgive me for what I did to you at Winchester. I cannot die without peace. Signed, Drummond."

Bates leaned back in his overstuffed chair. He thought for a long time, then he reached over and drew in front of him the telegram pad of the British Empire, and he wrote out a three-word answer: "Cannot forgive. Bates."

Now Bates was a leader in the Church of England, a declared Christian, and so was Drummond for that matter. The tragedy was that for all of those years, from the early thirties to the middle of the nineties, Drummond carried the memory of the hurt that he had inflicted on his friend, but only at the point of death could he say, "God, forgive me" and then write to his friend personally and confess what he had done.

Bates was a dignified leader of the British Empire, a great leader in the church, and a Christian of recognition, yet he could not bring himself to apply the atonement of the cross to a relationship and forgive a person who needed to die in peace.

The Burden of the Unforgiven

As Leonardo da Vinci painted _The Last Supper_, he was nursing a grudge toward a friend. To get back at him, he used the friend's face as a model for Judas. Then he said, "There! Now the whole world will know what kind of person he is." Afterwards, when he tried to paint the face of Christ he couldn't do it. It was only later, when he took his friend's face off of Judas and put another face there, that he was able to paint the face of Christ.

What about you? Have you been carrying the heavy, heavy burden of things that you have never forgiven? Failures of the past or things that have been said and done to you?

When Friedrich Wilhelm, monarch of Prussia, lay dying, his chaplain came to him and said, "You must forgive your enemies." Friedrich's wife was standing by. "My greatest enemy is your brother," he said to his wife. "After I die, will you tell him that I forgave him?"

The chaplain interceded and said, "Why not do it now?"

"No, after I die," he said, "my wife will tell him. That will be safer."

Why do we hold back on giving to others what Christ has given to us?

There will be no peace in our lives until we fulfill the righteous demands of God. And when we fail to seek His forgiveness, there will be no peace in our lives until those who have hurt us have been forgiven by us and are cleansed.

We will cry, "Peace, peace." And there will be no peace.

But there can be peace. It can happen now! The peace of Jesus Christ, who atoned for our sins, can be the source of your forgiveness and provide the power for you to forgive others right now!

Prayer for a Forgiving
and Forgiven Heart

Blessed and loving Father, I ask You for a profound, fresh experience of repentance, forgiveness, and renewal so that I may be capable, through the indwelling power of Your Spirit, to forgive the people in my life. All-forgiving Lord, help me to stand at the foot of the cross until true repentance can take place. Motivate me with Your Spirit. Help me to be responsive. Give me the peace of a forgiven and forgiving heart. In the name of Your forgiving heart, who is Jesus Christ. Amen.

Chapter 6

PEACE IN LIFE'S PROBLEMS

*Peace I leave with you, My peace I give to you;
not as the world gives do I give to you. Let not your heart
be troubled, neither let it be afraid.*
—JOHN 14:27

I sat alone at my desk for hours thinking about the frantic people who had cried out to me for help. Like pressure cookers, their demanding lives were filled with too much to do, too many deadlines, too many people to care for, too little time to relax and replenish their spirits. Their problems had piled up, making them like rubber bands stretched to the breaking point. Every one of these people needed a fresh experience of Christ's peace for their problems.

I studied the passages of peace in both the Old and the New Testaments. I went over each one, pondering the meanings, and then I came to these words of Jesus. They seemed to leap off the page, gripping me with freshness as if I had never read or heard them before. "Peace I leave with you, My peace I give to you.... Let not your heart be troubled" (John 14:27).

It's amazing. The more I study history, the more I realize that many spiritual leaders in every period have passed through times when they rediscovered the meaning of things that they had been teaching and preaching to others.

I recall the moving experiences of the great preacher Dr. Robert William Dale of Carr's Lane Congregational Church in Birmingham, England, as he rediscovered the essence of what was the center of his faith. He had preached the resurrection Easter after Easter. He had explained it intellectually. He had communicated it in his pulpit over and over again. And then one Saturday afternoon before Easter Sunday morning, he was pacing back and forth in his study. All of a sudden it hit him. "Christ is alive!" he shouted. "He's really alive, and He's here! He's risen from the dead! Hallelujah!" And then he went into his pulpit to preach the resurrection as he had never preached it before. Here was a biblical scholar, a man who loved Jesus. And then one day he had a fresh experience of Christ. Suddenly it all became real to him!

Dr. Hudson Taylor, the great leader of the China Inland Mission, had run out of steam and energy, vision, and hope. He didn't know what to do. He was trying to help other people when he really needed help himself. He acknowledged his brokenness and said, "Lord, I'm exhausted working for You. Please work through me. Take over the China Inland Mission. Spread the gospel through me. I can't do it on my own strength." That was when Hudson Taylor experienced for the first time, he said, the deepening of the indwelling power of Jesus Christ—after he stopped trying to live and work on his *own* energy.

One of the greatest preachers of the nineteenth century, Charles Haddon Spurgeon, came to a difficult time in his life. He was ill, frustrated, and tired out from preaching the gospel. On his sickbed and about to give up, he had a fresh experience of Christ. The Lord gripped him and gave him fresh vision and hope. He returned to preach as he had never preached before.

A similar thing happened to me as I read the passage from John. I pictured the scene in the Upper Room the night before Christ's crucifixion. I saw the disciples frightened and uncertain about the future. I saw Jesus looking at them intently with love and compassion, wanting to pass on His legacy. Then I heard Him say, "Peace I leave with you, My peace I give to you; not as the world gives do I give to you. Let not your heart be troubled, neither let it be afraid."

It suddenly hit me. For years I had repeated those same words at every funeral service I'd ever done. "Peace I leave with you, My peace I give to you." I had seen the impact of those words of comfort and encouragement on the lives of troubled people. Now in the quiet I knew that Christ had said those words for me! I was gripped with the realization that Christ was offering *me* His peace. I could hear Him asking me, "Do you want a fresh gift of peace? It's here for you to receive."

He is actually telling us that the peace we read about in the Gospel record of His life is the same peace that you and I can receive, nothing less.

Confidence in God's Intervention

Let's take a look at that peace. Look at the context in which Jesus says, "Peace I leave with you, My peace I give to you." It's hard to imagine more difficult circumstances in which those words could be spoken. Jesus had taken a battering from the leaders of Israel—questioning, cross-examining, hostility, and anger. He could see in Peter's eyes the cloudy look of deception that would lead to defection and denial. He knew that Judas was betraying Him at that very moment. Talk about troubles! It was in the midst of this kind of terrible trouble that Jesus uttered these words about peace. How was He able to do that?

The answer lies in the fact that the peace of Jesus Christ was not based on His feelings but on the clear conviction that God is sovereign and all-powerful. In addition, Jesus lived with confidence in God's timely intervention. How else could He offer peace on the night before His crucifixion knowing the trials He would go through as He became the substitutionary sacrifice for the sins of the whole world!

To go into a battle like Calvary knowing that you have already won is something else, isn't it? Wouldn't it be wonderful if we could always live that way? We could, you know. God's peace is available to you and me today. Peace can be ours as soon as we begin living with the assurance that God's intervention will come on time, in time, and in the right way. We need only pray as Christ did, clearly acknowledging our dependence upon the Father.

Jesus also showed us how to depend on the Holy Spirit to work the miracles that we claim from the Father. Think about how Jesus would see someone who was ill and reach out His hand with the healing power of the Holy Spirit surging through it.

And Jesus promised, "Most assuredly, I say to you, he who believes in Me, the works that I do he will do also; and greater works than these he will do, because I go to My Father" (John 14:12). And He promised the power of the

Holy Spirit saying, "…and We will come to him and make Our home with him" (John 14:23).

Oh, how we take these astounding words for granted! The Savior of the world has offered to come to you and me and give us His peace. We need not remain impotent victims of our problems, fast-paced daily lives, or the forces of evil. Christ has given us an example of how to live, and His peace exists in the midst of it.

Here we have a true picture of the peace Jesus exemplified as He lived life as it was meant to be lived. Christ's peace was rooted in consistent prayer to the Father, confidence in the power of the Spirit, confrontation with Satan as the robber of peace, constant surrender to the Father's will, and complete trust in the Father's intervention. When we can visualize this picture, we are ready to realize the awesome assurance that this is exactly the same peace Jesus can give us by abiding in us today. We can become postresurrection homes for the living Christ!

Jesus went to the cross so that we might know we're forgiven and so that we could share with Paul this liberating confidence: "Having been justified by faith, we have peace with God through our Lord Jesus Christ" (Romans 5:1).

A Double-Edged Sword

The same Jesus who, on the night before He was crucified, said, "My peace I give to you," a few days before said, "Do not think that I came to bring peace on earth. I did not come to bring peace but a sword" (Matthew 10:34).

Does that seem like a paradox? It's not. The concept is quite simple really: The very one who gives us peace also troubles our false sense of peace. Herein lies one of the most important secrets for living through troubled times in the peace of God. I want to grip your mind with it. I don't want you to leave this chapter until you understand it.

It's because we have identified peace so much with our feelings and not with our convictions that we have a hard time realizing that the same Jesus who gave us eternal peace and the assurance of heaven, His presence, and His power is also in the people-transformation business. He will change us, and He will press us into those situations around us that need change. He'll put the painful needs of other people on our hearts. He'll unsettle us. He'll goad us and push us and keep us on the growing edge.

There was a little boy who came home from first grade with a great big star. His dad said, "We're so proud of you!" And the little boy said, "Yeah, Dad, I got the best star of all." His dad asked, "What was it for?" The little boy said, "Every day we have a rest period. We have to close our eyes and try to sleep. My teacher gave me a star for being the one who rests better than anyone else."

That's one star I don't ever want to receive! To belong to Jesus Christ means to be on the move. He will constantly press our hearts next to the heart of pain around us. He'll make us concerned about people who don't know Him.

He also puts this concept into the context of family relationships. "I did not come to bring peace but a sword" (Matthew 10:34), to set asunder father and son, mother and daughter, mother-in-law and daughter-in-law. And then He gets to the real issue: "He who loves father or mother more than Me is not worthy of Me…and he who loses his life for My sake will find it" (Matthew 10:37,39).

Jesus gives us His peace, and then He presses into our relationships, into our thinking and attitudes about the past, the present, and the future that rob us of peace. You see, He's raising up a great person in you and me. He wants us to be like Him and, therefore, He will not give us the peace of conformity, the peace of false calmness, the peace of placidity. He's up to exciting changes in you and me.

We're going to live forever. Christ wants to be quite sure of the kind of person who gets to heaven, and so He encourages and challenges us, constantly giving us opportunities to grow. It's His job description to get you and me into heaven as transformed people.

The author of Hebrews was right when he said that the Word of God is like a two-edged sword. When we read the Scriptures, there are times that they are unsettling. We learn more about God than we thought we were ever going to learn, and it reorients our whole understanding of life of history, and of the future. We also read about ourselves and learn what is the next step in our own growth.

The Great Inheritance

Jesus never gives us a problem that He won't help us solve. He never gives us a hurting person He won't help us heal. He will always sustain us in every situation. And if that's true, then you and I have some business to do with Him today. We need to be quite sure that we have received His wondrous legacy of peace. It would be a terrible thing to have received an inheritance check and never cashed it.

I've had the privilege of talking to a few people who have received great inheritances. I once searched all over

Philadelphia for a young man who had been left a great deal of money. He had been in a hostile relationship with his father. Even though he could have become a millionaire, he chose to live on the streets of Philadelphia because he didn't want to come home and sign the papers to claim what his father had left him.

Jesus has given us a great legacy for our problems. The bequest is yours and mine. Will you take it? If you do take it, I want you to know that after you have taken it, Christ will *take* you. At every stage of new peace there'll be new discoveries, and then He'll call you to move on. Nature abhors a vacuum. Jesus abhors the ruts of routine.

It's an awesome thing to fall into the hands of Jesus Christ. William Booth, the great leader of the Salvation Army, was startled awake one day with the realization of how he had fallen into the Savior's arms and how the Lord had given him the power to fulfill his dreams.

> I will tell you the secret: God has had all that there was of me. There have been men with greater brains than I, even with greater opportunities, but from the day I got the poor of London on my heart and caught a vision of what Jesus Christ could do with me and them, on that day I made up my mind that God should have all of William Booth there was. And if there is anything of power in the Salvation Army, it is because God has had all the adoration of my heart, all the power of my will, and all the influence of my life.

And what about you? Does God have all that there is of you?

The Timing of Answers to Our Problems

Some things are easier to surrender to the Lord than others. Take our schedules for instance. We pray about our problems and when our prayers are not answered according to the timing we desire, we become anxious. Waiting and wondering become excruciating. We become impatient with God.

The idea that there may be something to gain out of waiting seems preposterous. And when the waiting goes on "too long" we become alarmed. We steel ourselves against the possibility that there are deeper lessons to be learned while waiting for solutions to our problems. Our fondest hope is that the Lord will find some other means for our growth than making us wait for the resolution of our difficulties.

We have all been members of the same club—the "Lord, I want it done yesterday" club. What we fail to realize is that it's more than the immediate solutions to our problems that we need; we need the Lord Himself. Turning our lives over to the Lord's control is not easy. Praying about our needs is one thing; letting go of them is another. Turning our lives over to the Lord is often blocked by self-sufficiency and pride conditioned by years of practice at running our own lives. We turn to the Lord for help only when we run into a big problem we can't solve by ourselves. When His immediate solutions are not forthcoming, we often become angry and resentful.

If this is the problem that is compounding your problems, I encourage you to consider seriously your need to surrender to the Lord your whole life as well as your problems and to relinquish your determination to tell Him how and when the solutions should come. Trust the Lord. He's never early or late. The Lord solves your problems with His grace, love, and peace. He longs to give you a profound experience of His unqualified love. Often He chooses to wait rather than to bless you with immediate answers to your requests so that you can depend more fully on Him and His timing.

How Paul Found Peace
for His Problems

Finding peace in the midst of problems is the great discovery the apostle Paul made at a particularly difficult time in his life. Paul gives us the secret in 2 Corinthians. Here he ushers us into his inner mind and heart. One of the most dynamic Christians who ever lived opens himself with vulnerability and honesty to share his problems and the Lord's response to what seemed to be a long time of unanswered prayer.

Paul relates several levels of problems. Our desires to be exempt from trouble seem simplistic when compared to the list of difficulties Paul endured.

> Three times I was beaten with rods; once I was stoned; three times I was shipwrecked; a night and a day I have been in the deep; in journeys often, in perils of waters, in perils of robbers, in perils of my own countrymen, in perils of the Gentiles, in perils in the city, in perils in the wilderness, in perils in the sea, in perils among false brethren; in weariness and toil, in sleeplessness often, in hunger and thirst, in fastings often, in cold and nakedness—besides the other things.
> —2 CORINTHIANS 11:25-28

The apostle was proud of the fact that in all these things he had experienced the sustaining power of Christ's peace. Then he suffered a physical problem. There has been a great deal of conjecture about what it was. Some have suggested ophthalmia, a disease of the eyes, and still others have said it was malaria. We don't know for sure. Whatever it was, it drove the proud apostle to prayer.

"Concerning this thing I pleaded with the Lord three times that it might depart from me. And He said to me, 'My grace is sufficient for you, for My strength is made perfect in weakness' " (2 Corinthians 12:8-9).

The Lord's response that His grace was sufficient for Paul has been used as an excuse for "unanswered prayer" and even as a caution about the impropriety of praying about our problems at all. It is also frequently used as a justification for the idea that the Lord does not answer some of our prayers about the needs in our lives. When someone endures a long period of waiting, we say, "Don't be so discouraged. Look at the apostle Paul. He prayed and he didn't get his prayers answered!"

God's Sufficiency for Our Insufficiency

On the contrary, I believe the Lord did answer Paul's prayer. The answer was His grace. Paul did not have to take pride in human accomplishments or in his vision to establish the authenticity of his apostleship. Christ alone was to be his sufficiency. The Greek word for "sufficient" is _arkeî_, "to ward off danger, to protect." Most important, Christ's grace in Paul's life would be perfected in his weaknesses. Here the Greek word for "is perfected" is the present passive indicative of *teleioō,* "to finish, to accomplish a purpose or end."

Out of Paul's realization of his own insufficiency, he was opened to receive the sufficiency of Christ. As I have explained, Christ is grace—unmerited, unchanging, unqualified, and unmotivated love. No merit in the apostle earned that grace. Paul's admission of weakness made him capable of receiving grace and peace.

When the Lord said, "My grace is sufficient for you, for My strength is made perfect in weakness," He directly answered Paul's prayer. He met Paul's deepest need. Christ's grace alone was all the apostle needed. The pride that had become a false security stood in the way of deep communion with the Lord and, I think, made it difficult for Paul to receive the healing of his physical illness. When he realized anew that Christ's grace was the only basis for his status as a forgiven sinner, he could claim the healing of his body as he had so often claimed healing for others.

Paul's response to the Lord's gift of grace also must be carefully studied so we don't fall into the trap of justifying the lack of answers to our prayers about problems. Paul said, "Therefore most gladly I will rather boast in my infirmities, that the power of Christ may rest upon me" (2 Corinthians 12:9).

This is the salient concept Paul teaches us: Our confession of weaknesses is a prelude to receiving peace in spite of our problems. Pride in its very subtle forms lurks at the center of our unwillingness to trust Christ with our needs. His grace is the only antidote to that spiritual sickness. Pride will prompt us to pray with a double mind. We can want solutions, answers, and healing without really wanting the Lord. And whatever it takes to break the bind of pride—even the delay that seems to be unanswered prayer—will be used by the Lord to bring us to the place where we want Him even more than solutions. Until that point of surrender, we will block the peace that the Lord wants to give us.

Learning to Be Thankful for Our Problems

When we come to the point where we can be thankful for the problem that brings us to the end of our own strength and endurance, we will be that much closer to God's strength. Then we can experience the peace and joy of knowing that it is in the Lord's hands.

"That's fine for others," you may be tempted to say. "They need that experience of suffering to bring them to Christ. I have been a Christian for a while now. Why do I have to go through struggles? To keep me close to the Lord?" That question is asked of me so often wherever I go.

Really it's the wrong question asked in the wrong way. No, the Lord doesn't make life a struggle just to keep us open to His grace. Rather, we struggle whenever we begin placing our confidence in anything or anyone other than the Lord. When we realize we are in trouble, we cry out for His help. What seems to be a long waiting period of "unanswered prayer" is really the amount of time it takes for us to realize our need for the Lord as our only sufficiency.

Don't fall into the trap of becoming filled with panic about not being sufficient for the problems at hand. No one is sufficient. None of us has what it takes for the ever-changing, ever-increasing problems that life presents.

Don't stunt your growth in the Lord by keeping your life pared down to your human limitations. "I'll never be able to deal with that problem," we say. And we attempt to trim all the danger from our lives. But the moment we think we have been successful, we are confronted with more unexpected problems. If there is one thing we can count on in life, it's this: We will always have problems. When these are solved, we will have more, perhaps bigger than before.

The Lord wants us to be totally centered on Him, completely dependent on His grace alone, and unreservedly open to the flow of His Spirit within us. When we become self-sufficient with God as some kind of addendum to our own self-willed control, we most assuredly will be thrown by difficulties that come along. Problems will engulf us and scuttle our otherwise smooth-sailing ships. When self-sufficiency has a hold on us, our cries for the Lord will be contradicted by our reluctance to let go completely. Like Paul we will need healing for our pride and the resultant realization of just how far from Christ's peace we have drifted.

Constant Growth

With Christ's help, our problems will provide a constant source of growth. As Christians, we will never be able to rest easy at any level of development. I realized some time ago that every accomplishment in my life has always been followed by new problems that are far beyond my own human ability to face and solve. I've never had time to sit back and savor success. New and fresh challenges always kept me aware of my inability to cope without the Lord's intervention and strength. It was a great relief to accept, finally, that this is the way it's always going to be.

Support for the Journey

God's consistently awesome challenges force us to realize that we are insufficient without Him and that we need each other's support and prayers. Some of the senators who meet weekly for Bible study, mutual support, and prayer keep the following covenant expressing our dependence on the Lord and each other.

- We will begin each day with an unreserved commitment of our lives to Christ.
- We will invite Christ to fill us with His Spirit: our minds to think His thoughts, our emotions to express His love, and our wills to discern and do His will.
- We will focus on the specific opportunities and challenges in our relationships and responsibilities in the day ahead.
- We will surrender each of these to Christ and ask for supernatural power, wisdom, and guidance for our leadership.
- We promise to pray for each other by name, picturing each other, and asking for Christ's special empowering. During the day, as we are brought to each other's minds or learn of special needs, we will accept these as nudges to intercede for each other.
- We will end the day with a time of reflection on how the Lord blessed and empowered us so that gratitude and praise will conclude each day.

Each time one of us comes close to victory over some soul-sized problem, someone says, "Now that the Lord's won that battle, get ready for the next one!" And sure enough, usually in the next week or two, some problem or opportunity develops to convince us of our insufficiency and His amazing sufficiency for our needs. This has been a growing experience for all of us. We have gained the peace of knowing we don't have to attempt the adventure in Christ alone.

I recall the story told to me by former U.S. Senator from Florida, Connie Mack, about the life-changing moment when he learned the secret of allowing God to lead him step-by-step through life's adventure:

> "I was attending a funeral service for the wife of a friend when it hit me. As I sat there, I realized that doing God's will is not the pursuit of the grand but rather the pursuit of His will one day at a time, one moment at a time. I knew right then that I needed to allow God to guide me one step at a time so I could eventually get to where He wanted me to be in my life. Then I could be at peace.
>
> "It was a life-changing moment for me—a radical departure from my previous life of management by objective and goal setting. State a goal, target an objective, and then pursue it. Since that day, I have pursued God one step at a time without worry or wondering where it may lead me. I ask God to help me to do what is right, what is His will at that moment, and then life takes care of itself."

The Adventure of Attempting the Impossible

When we live our lives in God's sufficiency, we open ourselves to the flow of the Lord's power to accomplish what He wants to do through us. And the Lord constantly wants to press us beyond our human capabilities. It is in that slippery interface between who we are and who He calls us to be that we discover His power and peace. In drawing on God's power, we can persistently take risks with raw faith. The greater the risk the more faith, daring, and peace we will receive. Encounters with Christ spur people on to attempt the impossible!

By trying to be sufficient, we cut ourselves off not only from the flow of the Lord's power to accomplish the humanly impossible things He wants to do through us, but also from His perfect peace.

Letting Go of Your Problems

No matter what problems you are facing now or will face in the future, remember this: "Peace I leave with you, My peace I give to you" means, "I'm with you all the way. I'll never let you go. Sure, you're going to have problems. There are times that'll you'll ache and hurt, but you haven't lost your peace or My power. You're just moving on to a deeper peace and a greater power than ever before."

Continued growth in God means committing our problems to Him and discovering the dynamics of what He is ready to reveal to us. When those truths become fresh and new, life really gets exciting.

As I mentioned in chapter 3, _The Peace That Comes from Knowing God_, once you make a commitment, the whole universe conspires to accomplish it. In a deeply Christian sense, once we make a commitment to live in Christ's sufficiency, the Lord and all the angels and archangels and all of the forces and powers of our Lord conspire together to help us accomplish it. Give your problems to God. Do it today! You'll be on your way to deeper peace than you've ever experienced.

PRAYER FOR GOD'S HELP
WITH PROBLEMS

Gracious living Lord Jesus Christ, I bless and praise You for taking me into Your care. You've called me to be Your disciple and have taken the responsibility for the shaping of my mind and character and will. You have determined to make me like You, and You're not going to give up on me. Thank You for giving me the kind of peace that sustains me in the midst of all my problems. Be with me, Lord, as I commit to receive Your eternal peace and do everything I can to share it with others, in Your peace-infusing name. Amen.

Chapter 7

PEACE—OUR GUARD AND GUIDE—A PRESCRIPTION FOR WORRY

Be anxious for nothing, but in everything by prayer and supplication, with thanksgiving, let your requests be made known to God; and the peace of God, which surpasses all understanding, will guard your hearts and minds through Christ Jesus.
—PHILIPPIANS 4:6-7

I awoke with an uneasy feeling. There was no apparent cause that I could identify. It did not go away as I showered, dressed, and ate breakfast. In fact, the mood had increased by the time I started the day's work. I sat at my desk wondering what was wrong, trying to get in touch with the feelings inside me.

In my morning prayer, I asked God to help me. Then in the quiet time, He finally revealed the cause of the alarm signal ringing in my soul. Over the previous month I had collected a bag of unresolved situations. All of them were on hold—waiting for solutions, answers from people, and the working out of some unfulfilled visions I felt God had put on my agenda. Impatience engulfed me. Suddenly I realized that

I was worried about the future. How would things work out? Would there be solutions? What would I do if my dreams didn't come to fruition?

Ever feel that way? Perhaps you're worried right now as you read this. How are you feeling about your future right now? Confident? Patient? Anxious? Uncertain? Worried? Panicked? Maybe someone you love is suffering from the worry syndrome.

There are times when we all get hit with a blast of anticipation and worry about the future, often when we least expect it. Our personal and professional futures seem to be up for grabs. There may be little concrete evidence that this could be true, but the uneasiness persists. The problem is not in the unknown future circumstances, but in us.

Though I could not have said it that morning, I can write it now. I'm glad it happened. Going through this spasm of emotional frustration put me in touch with what many people live with every day of their lives. I talk to worried people nearly every day. They share their anxieties with me in counseling sessions. I listen, probe for deeper understanding of their fears, and encourage them to talk to me until they know what they want to say to God in prayer. I have learned that the most important step in spiritual counseling is to help people spread out their needs before God, surrender control, and ask for His guidance, discernment, wisdom, and power. A sure sign that people have let go and have trusted God with their worries is that they have received the supernatural gift of peace.

Throughout our conversations in this book we have honestly confronted the things that rob us of peace. In this chapter I want to talk about worry as a major disturber of peace and claim a promise of Jesus and an admonition of the apostle Paul as two aspects of the secret to banish the thief of peace—inordinate worry.

Worry is thinking turned toxic, the imagination used to picture the worst. The word _worry_ comes from a root meaning "to choke or strangle." Worry does choke and strangle the creative capacity to think, hope, and dream. It twists the joy out of life.

The disturbing truth is that worry changes nothing except the worrier. The distressing habit of worry is impotent to change tomorrow or undo the past. All it does is cause anxious days and sleepless nights. William Inge was right: "Worry is the interest paid on trouble before it becomes due." Henry Ward Beecher put it bluntly: "Worry is rust on the blade." It renders us incapable of cutting our way through what is bothering us.

The Worry Habit

Over the years in messages and books, I've tried to communicate my conviction that worry is a low-grade form of agnosticism. _Agnostic_ is a compound word meaning "not to know." It certainly compounds our problems! Agnosticism is rooted in uncertainty about the Lord's ability to meet our needs. And it is nourished by fear that there may be problems and perplexities in which we will be left alone—out on a limb without God! A terrible loneliness results from prolonged worry. It's facing life's eventualities by ourselves, on our limited strength. Worry makes us feel that we are victims, powerless to change the nightmares we conjure up in our imaginations.

Worry becomes a habit, a repetitive pattern that ends up as an addiction. When there's little to worry about, we thrash about looking for something we can worry over.

Help Is Here

Is it possible to receive peace to overcome the syndrome of worry? Yes. Think of it this way: When we worry, we exercise our ability to care without expectation of Christ's intervention with His supply of peace and power. If worry is caused by feeling alone in the face of imagined or real fears and by a feeling of having to work out solutions without help, then the Lord's peace is the only lasting hope for our battles with worry.

Remember the thesis we're developing in this book. Christ Himself is our peace. All our efforts to establish peace in our thinking without Peace Himself will be futile. Just as we did for our problems, we must ask for the indwelling Spirit of Christ in times of worry.

Sometimes I get caught in the downward spiral of worry before I remember to ask for the supernatural endowment of peace. I'm not alone. Seldom have I talked to people troubled with worry who specifically ask for the anointing of Christ's peace. I've found that when I start to worry I need to think creatively about how to act on Jesus' admonitions. Worry is immobility. The Lord, on the other hand, wants to move us off of dead center.

How We Can
Stop Worrying

Paul knew how to experience Christ's peace in the midst of worry. In a marvelously uncluttered and straightforward statement, the apostle tells us what to do when anxieties pile up and we need the peace of God to help us cope. "Be anxious for nothing, but in everything by prayer and supplication, with thanksgiving, let your requests be made known to God; and the peace of God, which surpasses all understanding, will guard your hearts and minds through Christ Jesus" (Philippians 4:6-7). How's that for a prescription for anxiety relief?

Paul's advice is that instead of anxious rumination over our worries, we should come to God in prayer. The present imperative of the apostle's prohibition could be, "Stop being anxious." How can we do that when we are deeply disturbed by worry? Simply by channeling that same concern into prayer. Note that Paul combines prayer and supplication. Prayer involves adoration for who God is in His glory and grace. Supplication—that is, specific requests related to particular needs—follows.

A personal word to you, my reader and friend. We all have worries. I have mine and you have yours. The good news is that God knows and cares. The amazing thing is that He pays attention to each of us as if there were only one of us. He loves us so much He wants us to talk to Him about what's troubling our minds and then ask for His interventions to bring us peace. Often He waits to release peace until we talk to Him in prayer.

The apostle Paul tells the Philippians and us that the peace of God is no marshmallow noun. It's active, dynamic. As a matter of fact, in Romans 16:20, the apostle Paul tells the Christians at Rome that peace will put Satan under their heels. Peace—not just the God of peace or the God who will give you peace and then leave you to struggle with Satan's power on your own—but the peace of God will put Satan under your heel.

Thanksgiving in Advance

Paul encourages us to make our supplications with thanksgiving. If we can't thank God for hearing us and for the answer in advance of receiving it, we haven't really committed it to Him. A similar message from Paul was sent to the Thessalonians stressing the importance of thanksgiving. "Rejoice always, pray without ceasing, in everything give thanks; for this is the will of God in Christ Jesus for you" (1 Thessalonians 5:16-18).

Thanksgiving is the ultimate relinquishment. To pray, "Thank You, God, for providing what You know is best for me and all concerned," is the secret of powerful supplication. We must surrender our efforts to control. Remember that the root of the Hebrew word *commit* means "to roll over." When we commit our worries, we roll them off our weak and trembling hands into the mighty hands of God. "Commit your works to the LORD, and your thoughts will be established" (Proverbs 16:3).

Pause for a moment to reflect. Have you been able to thank God in advance for His answers to your present worries—on time and in time for your ultimate good? Chances are you're still clutching onto whatever you've not been able to thank God for in advance. I've certainly discovered that in my life. When I thank God in advance for His answers, I know I really have let go. How about you? Can you thank Him right now? I need to and so do you. I thank God for hearing our relinquishing gratitude at this very moment.

What God Will Do for You

Now relish what God will do for you and me. God's peace "which surpasses all understanding, will guard your hearts and minds through Christ Jesus" (Philippians 4:7). We come to God with supplication coupled with thanksgiving, and He comes to us through Christ to give us His superlative peace.

This perfect peace cannot be contrived by our understanding alone. Paul is not suggesting that we can't comprehend the wonder of this invincible peace; it is a gift we can receive. As we have learned, the peace of God is the Spirit of Christ. His shalom, harmony, wholeness, well-being, and knitting together of what is fragmented or frayed in us comes to us when we invite Christ to dwell in our hearts and minds. It is a supernatural, divine implant.

The Greek word for *guard* in the phrase "guard your hearts and minds" is *phrouresei*, the future active indicative of *phroureō*, "to see before, to look out." God's peace is like a sentinel who guards our lives. The word also means "to garrison, to watch out for, to protect." Paul knew the Philippians could picture the Roman soldiers who walked the ramparts to defend the Roman colony city of Philippi. They also could identify the guards who surrounded the Roman dignitaries as they moved about the city.

Christ's guarding of peace is within us on round-the-clock duty, watching for approaching danger, sounding the warning signal, defending us from anything that could produce panic in our hearts or worry in our thinking.

Peace-Guarded Hearts and Minds

Just how does the indwelling Spirit of Christ's peace guard our hearts and minds? We live in a world that is fraught with worry, sick and troubled with disturbed people, confused values, distorted thinking, and evil influences. To empower us to live in this kind of culture the Spirit of the living Christ comes within us to assure us of the true meaning and value of the peace He lived, died, arose again, and ever lives to make possible.

Think of the dynamic elements of true peace: the assurance that we are loved and forgiven, the promise of healing for our painful memories, the vanquishing of our fears, the confidence that we will be guided each step of the way, the quiet satisfaction that comes with knowing our needs will be met in a way that helps us grow and glorifies God, the certainty that our dying will not be an ending, and the anticipation that we will live forever.

These, for openers, are facets of the peace that the Spirit of Christ brings to us. They enlighten our minds, provide emotional health and volitional courage. Every part of the inner being is transformed by Peace Himself. With His strength we can have what it will take to survive in the world. He will protect us from anything, any temptation, any involvement, any relationship that could keep us from realizing our full potential as His disciples.

Peace Himself can walk the corridors of our minds examining what we hold in our memories and in our imaginations. He can serve as the monitor of our thinking brains, the implementing faculty of our wills, and the source of our emotional health. Peace in our hearts begins with Christ's healing love.

Christ-Motivated Love for Ourselves

People cause much of the pain and distress in the world. When we are the cause of the problem, it's healthy to be able to admit it. But if we make ourselves responsible for everyone else's slights and oversights, we will become anxious about life. Hostility against ourselves will develop into a habitual, conditioned pattern of response. Only Christ can help us own our real failures, disown them in His forgiveness, and press on. Then we can acknowledge the failures of others and forgive them as we've been forgiven.

Healthy, Christ-motivated love for ourselves is expressed in creative self-expression. When we feel good about ourselves, we are able to communicate our needs and allow the people around us to help us. We are able to express our feelings without attacking people or blaming them; thus, we free them to respond to us without becoming defensive. Conversely, the feeling of not being loved results in diminished self-esteem. This in turn can lead us to suppress our emotions. Unexpressed emotions can fester into hostility and anxiety.

Anxious worry is eccentricity—being ex-centric or away from the center. When we suppress our negative emotions about ourselves, we are in effect taking punishment into our own hands. Since we have not learned to vent our anger creatively, we invert it on ourselves. There's a great difference between being sacrificial lovers of people and sacrificing ourselves for our own and others' failures. The one is self-abandonment, to which we are called as Christians; the other is merely self-blame.

The Spirit of peace wants to take us back over the years in order to heal those debilitating worries that have depleted our self-images and developed the anxious syndrome of self-condemnation. He exposes them to us if we are willing. Then He heals them with assuring love. We are given Christ-esteem and perfect peace. That radically changes how we think about the people around us and allows us to make a difference in society.

How to Express Christ's Love

Before our worries rob us of peace and turn into toxic anxiety, our challenge is to ask the Lord to clarify how we are to express His quality of love to others and to ourselves. Most every situation about which we worry is related to concern about a person or group of people. Thus, we must ask:

- Who needs to receive the Lord's mercy through me today?

- To whom can I give an undeserved break?

- Which of my worries are caused by judging others or condemning them?

- Am I holding any grudges?

- Who in my life needs me to be as generous in caring as the Lord has been to me?

Anyone, anything, any situations come to mind? The measure that we use for the overflowing blessings the Lord gives us will determine our ability to receive the peace He wants to give to us. Hurtful memories, unrelenting judgments, any people we've written off, or any guidance from the Lord to do good that we have delayed or flat-out denied will cause us worry and block our capacity to know, feel, and enjoy peace.

The Rule of the Peace Umpire

The overflowing of God's blessings is also the theme of Paul's epistle to the Colossians. In his message about how to live a new life in Christ, Paul gives an amazing admonition about peace: "And let the peace of God *rule* in your hearts, to which also you were called in one body; and be thankful" (Colossians 3:15). The peace of God is the palpable peace we receive through the indwelling Christ as the Father's gift.

The remarkable, salient thrust of this verse is the Greek word *brabeuétō*, from the verb *brabeuō*, to act as an umpire. It is the word used for an umpire who makes decisions on matters of dispute or priority. Just as an umpire settles questions in athletic events, so peace is the deciding factor in all our personal and interpersonal affairs.

Now what does this have to do with our worries? Everything! Christ, who is our peace (Ephesians 2:14), acts as the umpire of our lives. He helps us evaluate all attitudes and actions on the basis of whether they will maintain peace. He who is peace is the peacekeeper in our hearts. There are things we are tempted to say or do which will create worrisome turmoil in our inner beings. Christ rules them out. On a daily basis we can ask our umpire, "If I do this, will it rob me of peace?" Or "Will I have peace of soul if I welcome these thoughts and attitudes as guests in my mind?"

Most important of all, we can ask Christ, our indwelling umpire, to help us deal with our worries. He can call, "Three strikes! You're out!" to lots of things not worthy of our fretting. He also can call "Home safe!" for any legitimate concerns about which creative thought guided by Him can lead to actions He wants us to do.

Paul reminds us that we are called to live in peace with other believers. As we have noted, most of our worries deal with what people close to us have done or have failed to do. Relational peace means "to bind together, unify into an integrated oneness." Christ as arbitrator can help us sort out our differences with people. Instead of worthless worry, we can dare to ask Him to rule on our behavior as well as whatever distresses us about others. Only Christ can help us see ourselves honestly and others as they really are with their strengths and weaknesses.

Note the emphasis on the little word *let* in the phrase "Let the peace of Christ rule in your hearts." The imperative admonition is strong because we do have a choice. In the midst of worry we can choose to perpetuate the anxiety or ask for a ruling from our eternal umpire about whether what concerns us is worthy of further reflection or should be ruled "off base." More than a ruling, Christ gives us strength to let go of our tight grip on our worries, commit them to Him, and open ourselves to an inflow of fresh peace.

Worry never changed anything; Christ, the peace umpire, changes us and then everything else.

Six Ways to Prevent Anxious Thinking

Without missing a beat, Paul goes on in the fourth chapter of his epistle to the Philippians to show us six ways that Peace Himself can guard and guide our thinking from the toxic worry syndrome. He fills our minds with things which are good and deserve praise.

> Finally, brethren, whatever things are true, whatever things are noble, whatever things are just, whatever things are pure, whatever things are lovely, whatever things are of good report, if there is any virtue and if there is anything praiseworthy—meditate on these things.
>
> —PHILIPPIANS 4:8

These six adjectives provide a basis for peaceful thinking and creative decisions.

Here is a six-way test to see if your thoughts are guided by Christ and filled with His peace of mind.

Are they true? Truth Himself (John 14:6) has the right to ask. He is the truth about God, about how life was meant to be lived, about the moral absolutes of God in the commandments and the ethics for the elected—those chosen, called, and cherished as God's people. Untruth, thinking about things which degrade rather than what can be revered as valued by God, will eventually rob you of your peace.

Are they noble? The word in Greek means "venerable, inviting reverence, worthy of adulation." Does a thought produce reverence? Filling our minds with reverent praise for the natural world, the wonder of human personality, and the dignity of each person enables peace. When we think of people as gifts from God, we treat them with reverence. Life itself is seen as a privilege. It's a precious delight to be alive!

Are they right? There's no peace of mind without doing what is just. To be justified with God is to be right with Him. Christ reminds us of what He has done for us through the cross. As justified people, Christ can help us discern what is the righteous thing to do. He will never lead us to think about doing anything that will separate us from God. Righteousness is not a set of rules but a right relationship with God through faith. Any thought that disturbs that relationship will drain away our peace. Thoughts of self-justification or self-righteousness deny our status as loved and forgiven people.

Are they pure? The indwelling Christ exposes anything which pollutes the authentic. Spiritual purity requires that we *will* to do God's will; anything that causes us to give loyalty to a false god and anything that demeans the dignity of people will destroy our peace. Fantasizing in thought what we would not do in action will eventually drain away our peace. This includes thinking of people as sex objects as well as using our imaginations to conjure up actions which deny absolute honesty. Clean thoughts lead to veracity and virtue. Jesus said, "Blessed are the pure in heart, for they shall see God" (Matthew 5:8).

Are they lovely? Do your thoughts instigate love and actions of love? There are thoughts that produce loving relationships and generous giving of ourselves to others in words and deed. Christ Himself generates this quality of love. He generates the power to live out His new commandment to love others as He has loved us: "A new commandment I give to you, that you love one another; as I have loved you, that you also love one another. By this all will know that you are My disciples, if you have love for one another" (John 13:34-35).

What's new about that commandment? It is a call to love without qualification. The strength or weakness, adequacy or inadequacy of the recipient is not the motivation. Christ guards our thinking by keeping our thoughts free of manipulative love and guides us to say and do lovely things to all people. Christ places people on our agendas and helps us to communicate His amazing love.

Are they worthy of Christ's affirmation? Do you meditate on whatever is praiseworthy? Are your thought patterns worthy of Christ's praise? Are they excellent by His standard of what is constructive for our thoughts? Have you given Him control of your thought habits?

Paul follows this six-way test of thinking that enables peace of mind with a bold personal witness of how Christ garrisoned his mind and heart and guarded his thought and emotional life. "The things which you learned and received and heard and saw in me, these do, and the God of peace will be with you" (Philippians 4:9). Sounds a bit arrogant at first doesn't it? And yet, the apostle found the secret of peace during anxious times. It worked for him during his trouble-some ministry in Philippi, and it was working for him in prison in Rome while he wrote this epistle.

Paul's Formula

Do you have a formula for living with peace of mind and heart that you wish everyone shared? I can't think of a better one than Paul has given us:

- Bring your anxieties to the Lord.

- Surrender them to Him.

- Invite the Lord into your thoughts and feelings and accept His peace-infusing presence.

- Welcome Him as guard to ward off anxious thinking and emotional responses that will diminish your peace.

- Consistently take the six-way test for creative thinking.

- Share with others the secret of living with the peace you have found.

PRAYER FOR PROTECTION
AGAINST ANXIOUS WORRY

Dear Lord of Peace, thank You for Your love and forgiveness. Help me to identify the people who need to receive Your mercy through me today. I surrender my worries to You and ask for a fresh inflow of Your peace that I may be anxious for nothing. I invite You into my thoughts and feelings. Guard them. Make them true, noble, right, pure, lovely, and worthy of Your affirmation. Thank You in advance for the answers to my prayers and for Your willingness to remain my personal guardian with Your round-the-clock protection from the worry habit. Amen.

Chapter 8

PEACE IN THE MIDST OF PAIN

"For I will restore health to you
and heal you of your wounds," says the LORD.
—JEREMIAH 30:17

The earphones were placed on my head as I lay in the intensive care unit at Bethesda Naval Hospital. A cassette tape with inspiring music and Scripture verses was turned on as I began to return to consciousness. The first words I heard after the six-hour open-heart surgery were Jeremiah 30:17: "For I will restore health to you and heal you of your wounds."

"Say it again, Lord," I mumbled with parched lips. And, as if in direct response, the verse was repeated on the tape.

It was God's personal word to me in the midst of excruciating pain and discomfort after the traumatic quadruple bypass surgery. My rib cage had been sawed open and my heart stopped while my blood circulated through the heart-lung machine and four cholesterol-clogged arteries were replaced with blood vessels taken from my right leg and my left mammary artery. As the surgery was completed, my rib cage was drawn back together, tubes were placed in my chest for drainage, and the incision was expertly closed.

In the intensive care unit, my heart was monitored and the pain level carefully watched. And yet with all the medication, I still felt the pain resulting from the traumatic, invasive surgery.

Jeremiah 30:17 became my survival verse. Repeatedly, the words passed from the tape down my auditory nerve and were transmitted to my brain and into my very soul. Profound peace flooded my entire being—mind, soul, and body.

Why Do We Suffer?

God is good. We all know that. And yet how often do you wrestle with the seeming contradiction that God *is* love, but tragedies still happen? We all get sick from time to time. We all have pain. No one is exempt. Some of us endure physical pain, others emotional trauma and uncertainty; still others suffer from the effects of interpersonal conflict. We've all experienced pain from the loss of a loved one, the loss of a cherished dream, the loss of a hope that we have held in our hearts. We all routinely face the pain that comes with disappointment.

In our more lucid moments, we reflect on the fact that God created this world to be free, and in this free world bad things can and do happen. People make wrong choices, disrupt relationships, cause havoc in their communities. Sin and evil exist.

But when something happens to us—when pain, natural calamity, and the collusive forces of evil bombard us personally—we say, "God, how could You have allowed it?" It's because we believe that God is love that we find it difficult to understand why He allows pain into our lives. If we didn't think of the fact that He is love, we wouldn't be troubled. We could be among the atheists who say, "There is no God. It's all chance anyhow. What difference does it make?"

But you see, we can't have it both ways. For example, what would life be without gravity? Now, I'm thankful that gravity is at work right now because you're probably sitting down to read this book, and I hope you stay seated for a few minutes more until you finish this chapter. But it would take an effort to stand up because you're being held down by gravity. And I'm thankful that there's order in our universe because of the force of gravity that holds things together. But there are times when I haven't been happy about gravity. I've had loved ones and friends go down in plane crashes. That's when I want it both ways. I want to keep the airplane up, but I want gravity to hold everything else together.

Very often I've seen fire rage across a mountainside in southern California. Now I love the warmth of a fire, and I like the energy produced by the furnaces of industry, but I don't like fires that destroy. I don't like fires that are indiscriminate and burn houses with families and small children. I want it both ways.

People cause most of the suffering in the world. But do we want to get rid of them all? How would you like to have life without people? We want it both ways. We want people, but we don't want the things that some of them do.

Now God made a very profound decision when He created this world and placed humankind in it. He didn't make us puppets. Want to be a puppet? Want some strings attached to you that control what you do and what you say? Or do you want to be a person, called by God to be His person, but nonetheless given free will to choose to return His love and to love Him?

God's Suffering

God came into the midst of history, revealed His loving and forgiving heart, and showed us that He suffers with us. On the cross, His own Son died for the sins of the world. If we really focus on that truth, none of us can ever say that we suffer alone. God is with us in our pain! And now suffering takes on an entirely different meaning. Instead of our Father being against us—an enemy—He's with us, suffering with us, aching with us, helping us to endure the pain and to make the choices that are necessary.

In the midst of pain, we sometimes find it very difficult to accept what seems to be the indiscriminate management of God in the universe. We want to be darlings of the Almighty. We want Him to deal with us differently than He deals with others. And yet, He deals with us by loving and forgiving us, guiding and directing us, filling us with His own Spirit, and protecting us from thinking that we are alone and without His guidance and direction.

God as a Good Parent

I'll never forget a time when my oldest son, Scott, slipped while playing goalie on a soccer team. As a result of being trampled by an opponent, he received an injury which required fusing his lower back. On the sidelines, I wanted to rush onto the field. My friend caught me and said, "Don't you go in. You'll ruin that boy. He's got to fight his own battles."

Suddenly I caught a sense of what it must be like for God to give us complete freedom. And yet He constantly intervenes and works with our failures, challenges, and difficulties to bring good out of perplexity so we can say with the apostle Paul, "And we know that all things work together for good to those who love God, to those who are the called according to His purpose" (Romans 8:28). In the Greek it is God who is the subject of the sentence. God works things out. Things don't just work out!

We are children of God; we're destined for heaven, and nothing in our physical, relational, or situational suffering can separate us from Him.

Have you ever met someone who never knew any difficulties? Never had any suffering? Any disturbances? Everything came his or her way. Ever met a person like that? People like that usually seem irresponsible to me. Oh, give me someone who has faced the toughness of life, who has dared to go through the pain and the agony trusting God each step of the way. And when we dare to trust Him, giving thanks even for the pain, He transforms us, and while He's transforming the suffering, He's making us into pure gold. You see, God wants us to live with Him forever, and He's pretty concerned about the kind of person who's going to go to heaven. So along the way He uses everything that happens for our development. He shapes us and molds us, making us into the people He wants us to be.

Would you really want it any other way? A life without choice? A life without people who disturb you? A life that never has any pain? A life that is always easy? I don't. More than 50 years of living with the Savior has taught me that

He is faithful and that He takes over the management of our hearts. As we discussed in chapter 7, *Peace—Our Guard and Guide*, He walks the ramparts of our hearts, warding off anything that will destroy us or hurt us, using everything to make us into great people.

Depression

Sometimes when bad things happen to us we feel like we've been cut off from the peace of God. We start with feelings of self-pity. Then we turn blame and anger in on ourselves. Impression without expression becomes depression. Finally with the anger that we feel, we become depressed and life becomes anxious. God can save us from this scenario if we will but discover the wonder that He can give us His peace in the midst of it.

The gift of peace came to me in the midst of a minor depression that typically comes with the recovery from massive heart surgery. I sensed a supernatural peace that gave me patience with myself when my progress seemed slow. In the first weeks of recovery I often felt down for no apparent reason. With each recurrence I had to stop, remember the promise I'd received in Jeremiah 30:17, and claim Jesus' assurance of peace.

When I would wake up at night and be unable to sleep, I would ask the Lord to stay my mind on Him. (See chapter 2, *How to Have Consistent Peace.*) Then perfect peace would come flowing back into my mind and body. Divine peace doesn't take the pain away, but it does make it possible to endure it. When I would ask for the gift of peace, I found that my attention would be set free of worry, my muscles would relax, and my spirit would become calm and serene again. The peace I received was palpable. I could feel it surge against the pain.

Recovery

During the months of recovery, I got back on a regular and rigid daily exercise program: 20 to 30 minutes a day on the treadmill and 20 minutes on stationary weights. With warm-up and cooldown before and after, this made for an hour or more each day. I found this time good for the exercise of my mind and spirit as well as my body. I chose to reflect on the biblical promises for healing. I was able to reaffirm the basic conviction that Christ is the healing power of the world. This was coupled with a fresh awareness of the many kinds of pain from which we suffer. Physical pain can be excruciating, but so can emotional pain caused by the difficulties and discouragements of life. We all feel the pain of anguish over loved ones and friends who are distressed. No one is exempt from the pain of broken or strained relationships.

At the same time I was going through physical pain I was also dealing with the added emotional pain of worry about people I love. At first, I was resentful that I had to deal with the pain of the relational problems at the same time I was struggling with my own physical pain. Then it hit me: The same supernatural gift of peace I was given to deal with the physical heart pain was available to help me overcome spiritual heartache. Just as I had asked for the gift of peace in the intensive care unit of the hospital, so too I had to ask for Christ's peace for the intensive cares of my life.

Healing

Healing from major heart surgery is a long process. It involves not only the difficult first week after the operation but also the following weeks of recuperation and rehabilitation. I found that specifically asking for the gift of peace helped me in my battle with pain. Peace, as a fruit of the Spirit, was given with fresh anointing each day and many times during each day of my healing.

God's resounding "I will" promise assured me of healing. I had gone into surgery with the conviction that the Lord would guide the surgeon and that He would use the whole process to give me many more years to serve Him. Then too, I knew that whether I lived or died, I belonged to God. This life is just a small part of the eternal life I began when I became a Christian as a college freshman in 1948. But in the midst of my pain, the Jeremiah verse produced wondrous peace when I needed it most of all. Over and over I repeated the promise of restoration and healing. It was accompanied by Jesus' calming words, "Peace, be still."

In the New Testament the word *healing* is used to communicate the many aspects of wholeness we long to receive. The basic word is *sōzō*, the root from which both *save* and *salvation* come. It is also translated as "to make whole" or "to heal."

The author of Hebrews gives us a powerful "He is able" ascription about Christ, the healer of all kinds of pain: "Therefore He is also able to save to the uttermost those who come to God through Him, since He always lives to make intercession for them" (Hebrews 7:25). This verse also became a great source of strength and stability to me.

Save is a power word, one of the most powerful in the Bible. The entire sweep of its use in both the Old and New Testaments means "deliverance, wholeness, new life now, and eternal life forever." It is a cornucopia word which overflows with matchless treasure. Christ came to save us from our sins and complete our salvation on Calvary. He comes to live with us to make us whole in every facet of life. He heals us of spiritual estrangement and reconciles us for eternity. But He is not just concerned about eternal life; He also wants us to live the abundant life here and now. He saves to the "uttermost." That means He makes whole perpetually, He gives us His peace persistently, and He secures our eternal destination permanently.

As I was reclaiming this verse afresh during my recovery, I rechecked the Greek. Whom does Christ save to the uttermost? "Those who come to God through Him." The Greek word for "those who come," *proserchomenous*, is from a verb meaning "to come with consent." As I said before, we come in response to God's call, His invitation. We could not come if we were not first called; we could not decide to respond if Christ had not placed the desire within us. The gift of faith is given to us so we can come to Him and ask for the precious gift of peace. He invites us to come and gives us the courage to ask.

A second word for *healing* in the New Testament is *iaomai*. It is variously translated as "to heal" and "to make whole." It is used 22 times in the New Testament for physical healing. The word is also used for spiritual healing as in Christ's words quoting Isaiah 61:1 to declare His mission: "He has sent Me to *heal* the brokenhearted" (Luke 4:18). James in his epistle uses *iaomai* for healing of both physical and spiritual needs.

A third word used in connection with healing is *hugiēs*. In the Gospels it describes the state of being well or whole. This is the word used in Jesus' question to the man by the pool in Bethesda: "Do you want to be made well?" (John 5:6). The King James renders it "Wilt thou be made whole?" The same word is employed to describe what happened in Jesus' healing of the man with the withered hand. "Then He said to the man, 'Stretch out your hand.' And he stretched it out, and it was restored as whole as the other" (Matthew 12:13).

The Need for Our Cooperation in Healing

These two accounts of healing stress the need for our cooperation in the healing of pain. The man by the pool of Bethesda had been there for 38 years. The belief was that at divinely appointed times of mercy, an angel would descend and stir up the pool. The first person into the pool after the stirring of the water, it was believed, would be healed. When Jesus came to Jerusalem, He was drawn to this gathering place of human need. This man among the infirm particularly caught Jesus' attention. Jesus' question, "Do you want to be made whole?" indicates that perhaps the 13,870 days of waiting had caused the man to give up or that he had become so accustomed to being ill that he could no longer imagine himself well. The question reminds us that intense desire for Christ's help is a vital, necessary prerequisite for receiving His healing.

Applied to the many kinds of pain from which we suffer at times, only a personal encounter with the Great Physician can give us the courage to ask for peace and healing. The man by the pool had nothing but his need. It was in the majestic presence of the Master that he could confess that need and then follow Christ's command to rise up and walk.

Christ asks us, "Do you want to receive My peace in the midst of your pain?" The gift is given when Christ's desire to give and our desire to receive become one.

When we confess our needs, Christ is faithful. He takes us at our words of willingness. He heals us with love and forgiveness. He changes our attitudes about helplessness and releases His healing Spirit into our bodies. Our great need, above all needs, is for a relationship with the Prince of Peace. He is the inspiration of our knowledge that He is ready and able to help us. The stirring of desire to bring our pain to Him originates with Him.

When Christ responds to our prayers for peace, He says, "Go in peace." In the Gospel, this command means "go into peace." The full promise of health in body and soul is offered as an ever-increasing experience.

The Great Physician

The Lord wants us to realize His peace in every aspect of our lives. He enters our thinking brains to enable us to think His thoughts and to see things from His perspective. He heals our pain, our haunting memories, and changes our attitudes toward our future potential. He moves through our nervous systems, releasing innate healing resources to combat pain. He utilizes the pain-control medication prescribed and maximizes relief with His own healing Spirit. He gives us His strength. Our jangled nerves become calm, tensed-up muscles relax, and our reflexes stop twitching.

This I can say with greater conviction than ever before in my 50 years as a Christian: Christ is the Great Physician. As preexistent Christ prior to the Incarnation, He was the Father's healing power prayed for by priests and promised by prophets. As incarnate Messiah He exercised His healing powers: The blind saw; the lame walked; lepers were cleansed; the emotionally debilitated were set free. The early church became a healing community through which Christ continued His healing ministry. Now peace in the midst of pain is given when we ask the Healer to make us whole.

We grow into Christ's perfect peace. It usually doesn't happen all at once. One of the definitions of *peace* is "the knitting together of what is frayed and fragmented." The Lord knits our fragmented natures into harmonious functioning. He offers Himself in His present, persistent, and penetrating Spirit. We need to allow Him to take hold of more of us.

Often Christ's healing is debilitated in us by unconfessed sin, unloving attitudes to others, or uncommitted plans for our lives. What thoughts, habits, resentments, goals, ambitions have you tried to keep out of the reach of His healing touch? Often the answer defines your next step of growing *into* peace. Peace Himself and the gift of His peace can never be separated. They are one and the same.

The Promise

A few weeks after my bypass surgery, my good friends Jack and Anna Hayford visited me. We talked, sang, and prayed together. Once again I asked for the gift of peace for my pain.

I told the Hayfords about my experience of hearing the Jeremiah 30:17 promise on audiotape as I was coming out of the anesthetic after surgery. Later that evening, they told the hostess of the home where they were staying about my experience. She "happened" to have a copy of that verse in beautiful calligraphy framed on her wall. When the Hayfords left the next morning, she presented it to them saying, "Please give this to the chaplain for me." They did, and it now hangs on the wall of Mary Jane's and my bedroom right over the place where I sleep. Each night before I climb into bed, I reread the magnificent, perfectly timed promise: "I will restore health to you and heal you of your wounds." And He has!

Now I encourage you to come to the Great Healer for your gift of peace. Bring whatever brand of pain you have. The only suffering that can ever hurt you is that suffering which you clutch to yourself and don't give to the Lord. It is in times of pain that our Lord saves—heals to the uttermost. And that includes the pain you are experiencing right now. Don't just endure it. Invite the Lord to invade every part of your being with His peace. Whether it's physical suffering, emotional difficulties, a relational problem, or a painful memory from the past, give it to God. If you ask Him for help, He'll be there with you, and He'll turn it into growth. Have you ever done that? If not, you need to do it today. Now!

Prayer for Peace
in the Midst of Pain

Gracious Savior, You are able to save to the uttermost those who come to You. By Your invitation and instigation, I come to You. You have encouraged me to ask for Your perfect peace in the midst of my pain. The fact of Your presence, the assurance of Your love, and the conviction that You are the healing power of the world give me the courage to ask You to deal with my pain in a way that is ultimately creative for me. Take it away, heal its causes, subdue its distressing discomfort, or simply give me strength to endure. When physical pain or the pain of heartache bring me to tears, quiet me in Your love and wipe away the tears from my eyes. Give me peace, dear Lord. Amen.

Chapter 9

OUR UNBROKEN CONNECTION TO PEACE

But the fruit of the Spirit is...peace.
—GALATIANS 5:22

A key member of a senator's staff came by my office for a visit. He related his struggles to get ahead in the intensely competitive political world. Even though he was a Christian, he was still unable to find peace in his daily battle with stress. He wanted to leave the Hill, return to his state, and run for political office. I could feel yearning oozing from his whole being.

I asked, "Have you ever committed your life and professional plans to the Lord? Are you sure this is what He wants you to do?" I went on to explain that if he would surrender his future to the Lord's priorities, he could press on with His power and His peace. Our time of prayer was honest and open. His yearning had brought him to a turning point.

Now the young politician has won his bid for office, and he has done it with peace. Winning was not his goal. Today he is a servant leader under the Lord's orders and is filled with His peace.

Capitol Hill is a pressured atmosphere with highly motivated, ambitious, competitive people. Yearning pulses with seemingly unsatisfied persistence. There is an aching lack of peace in people who have never trusted the Lord with the control of their lives or asked Him for His plans for their lives. It has been my privilege to share with many of them the secret of the peace of a relinquished will.

"Why is it that sometimes I seem to lose the peace of Christ?" asked a senator with whom I meet weekly to discuss spirituality.

I explained to him the twofold blessing of abiding in Christ and inviting Christ to abide in us. The first assures us of all Christ did for us; the second accepts His indwelling presence.

I shared with my friend my own personal experience. It happened several years after my initial confession of faith in Christ. I was trying hard to be a good disciple on my own strength. Peace was an on-again, off-again experience dependent on my circumstances and surroundings, people's moods and attitudes, my success or failure. As a man "in Christ," I knew I was a recipient of salvation; I knew I'd been forgiven, that death had no power over me, and that I was alive forever, but I was missing out on the truth about Christ's greatest promise. I needed to invite Him to abide in my mind, emotions, will, and body. Christianity is not only life as Christ lived it or just living for Christ; it is Christ living in us!

We are meant to serve as vessels that contain and communicate Christ's life. Before realizing the power of the indwelling Christ, my life was a strenuous effort to be faithful and obedient. When I discovered I could not make it alone, He provided the power, motivation, and guidance. That's when His peace began to flow through me.

Direct Circuit to the Vine

Life in Christ does not run on a battery system—charged and then eventually running down again. I often wonder about Christians who say they need to get their batteries charged. Nice idea, but very wrong. We are made to operate on the direct-circuit principle: Christ keeps continuous contact and constant flow of the current of His Spirit. He doesn't strengthen us with booster cables when our batteries seem dead. Continuous communion with Him provides unvarying, nonfluctuating input because—as we have emphasized earlier—self-sufficiency is insufficiency, and Christ-sufficiency is all-sufficiency.

As noted in the previous chapter, in the Upper Room Jesus promised nothing less than His own peace. "Peace I leave with you, My peace I give to you; not as the world gives do I give to you. Let not your heart be troubled, neither let it be afraid" (John 14:27).

When Jesus and the disciples left the upper room, they made their way secretly through Jerusalem and passed the temple on the way to Gethsemane where Jesus would pray before He was arrested.

Over the main entrance to the temple was the exquisitely carved, gold-leafed symbol of the vine, branches, and grapes. It was firmly based on Old Testament Scripture and tradition. Israel was the Lord's "choice vine" (Jeremiah 2:21 NIV). I imagine that it was as they passed the temple precincts that Jesus said, "I am the vine, you are the branches." These are important words for us. Jesus is our vine, and His Spirit is the life-giving sap to produce His peace in His disciples—in you and me!

Lasting peace comes from an unbroken connection between us as branches and Christ as the true vine. Jesus said, "I am the vine, you are the branches. He who abides in Me, and I in him, bears much fruit; for without Me you can do nothing" (John 15:5).

The key word describing our dependence on the true vine as our source of peace is *abide*. The aorist active imperative of the Greek word in Jesus' teaching about the vine and the branches implies "keep on abiding." That's our only lasting source of limitless, free-flowing peace. *Abide* in this passage means "an unbroken connection" rather than "repose" as the word *abide* would suggest to us today. It strongly asserts the necessity of a constant, active connection between us and Christ's Spirit, the sap of His peace flowing into us as branches.

"Apart from Me you can do nothing," Christ says, driving home the point. There's no peace without Jesus Christ's Spirit abiding in us.

The Life Force Within

Paul's code name for the reproduction of Christ's character in us is *fruit of the Spirit*, the power of Christ's life force within us. In Galatians 5:22-23, the apostle holds up the precious cluster of characteristics produced by the Spirit through the unbroken connection: "But the fruit of the Spirit is love, joy, *peace*, longsuffering, kindness, goodness, faithfulness, gentleness, self-control" (emphasis added).

Peace is not something for which we strive—the result of enduring struggle. It is a fruit of the Spirit to be humbly received. Peace is not near, but here—within. It's not only Christ with us, but Christ in us. Peace is more than a state of freedom from jangled nerves; more than transient harmony, a temporary truce in relationships; more than a transitory calm in the storms of life. The peace of Christ is His own peace, the peace He had when He faced the cross and knew that the Father would reconcile the world through His death, the peace of the assurance that He would rise from the dead, the peace of knowing that a new creation would result with a new humanity of men and women in whom God would dwell.

The Magnificent Cluster

As I look at the cluster of the "fruit" of the Spirit, I see peace at the center. The fruit of love and joy is the source of peace and the other six are the substance of peace in action. It is important to emphasize that the word *fruit* is not plural. Paul does not talk about the fruits of the Spirit. That would seem to destroy the unity of the image to illustrate the power of Christ's life force within us. There's another reason: There is only one source from which Christlike character can flow—the Spirit of Christ Himself.

The fruit of the Spirit captivates all aspects of our human nature: intellectual, emotional, volitional, and behavioral.

Love

You may be surprised that I identify the fruit of love as intellectual. Too often we confuse love as having to do only with our feelings. We feel love, of course, but we first think love. We know we are loved because of the objective love given us in Christ. Divine love flows from Calvary into our souls. Our yearning to be loved unqualifiedly is satisfied. The fruit of love controls our thinking. We are able to love ourselves as loved by God through Christ. From that self-acceptance of and delight in ourselves as unique, special people comes the character trait of being a loving person who loves with the flow of the undiminishing Spirit of love.

Joy

The fruit of joy is an outward expression of that love. Joy is the result of being loved by God. When His grace and forgiveness penetrate through the thick layers of self-doubt and self-negation, we begin to feel the surge of joy. Here again, however, it is the fruit of joy surging through our emotions. There can be no joy without Christ living in us. After He explained about the unbreakable connection of the vine and the branches, Jesus said, "These things I have spoken to you, that My joy may remain in you, and that your joy may be full" (John 15:11).

Peace

In our mother's womb, we are given our souls. And each soul is endowed with a divine yearning for God. We are born physically with this longing that grows through the years. Often it is expressed in ways that do not satisfy. We yearn for significance, value, esteem, recognition, success, achievement, and material possessions. We yearn because we are never-to-be-repeated miracles of God, created to glorify Him. We will yearn, long, quest, and battle to achieve so that we can fill the empty vacancy within us. Why? Because we were created for a divine tenant who owns our souls. When He is in residence, the fruit—the manifestation of His presence—shows on our faces, in our actions, and in our characters. The fruit of peace is the "inbirthed" satisfaction of our divinely inspired yearning. Peace is the fruit of the Spirit that invades and transforms the will. If we think love and feel joy, we experience peace when we *will* to seek, discover, and follow the Lord's will for us. Peace grows in the fertile soil of a relinquished will.

Almost every day I talk with people—senators and staff alike—who yearn to discern God's will for their lives. Like the young politician we talked about earlier, their lack of peace often is due to decisions, plans, and goals that have never been relinquished to the Lord for His guidance. That's when I ask, "Is there some area, relationship, situation, or challenge in which you are either resisting or not seeking the Lord's will?" The fruit of peace flows again when we surrender our wills to His will.

In *The Divine Comedy*, Dante Alighieri put it directly: "In His will we find our peace." And Evelyn Underhill in her book *The Letters of Evelyn Underhill* struck the same note: "The real equation is not Peace equals satisfied feeling, but Peace equals willed abandonment." I would add "abandonment to the Lord's will." The fruit of peace grows through yieldedness to replace our yearnings.

All of the remaining fruit of the Spirit are expressions of peace in action. Note the progression: love grows in our thinking, joy in our emotions, peace in our wills, and long-suffering, kindness, goodness, faithfulness, gentleness, and self-control are grown in our behavior. If the first three deal with our relationship with God, the last six deal with how the indwelling Spirit helps us with our relationships with other people. All of these character traits comprise the reproduction of Christ's character in us.

Patience

The yearning of our souls, when possessed by peace, is controlled by the fruit of patience. Patience is rooted in an overarching conviction that the Lord is in control, that He is working out His purposes, and that we can live on His timing. We discover the shortness of time and the length of eternity. Our peace produces an active, confident trust that the Lord is on time, in time, and never one moment ahead of time for our times. Patience is knowing that the Lord has ruled what is best for us and that we will have it in His perfect timing. Peace is patience.

Kindness

Kindness is reaching out to those who fail or those who need acceptance. In the Bible, God's kindness was expressed in His persistent effort to reach people and enable them to return to Him. Jesus Christ was kindness incarnate, and now He instills this character trait in us. He enables us to become merciful, forgiving, sensitive, and caring. Instead of using people, we have the peace of knowing the Lord is using us to meet their needs.

Goodness

Goodness is the fruit of consistency. God is good. We are declared good because of our status as new creatures in Christ. The goodness of the Lord impels us to seek to do good works. There is congruity between what we believe and what we do. Hugh Latimer said, "We must first be made good before we can do good." When our restless yearning is transformed by Christ's peace and power, we long to know what is good for each person, situation, and challenge.

Faithfulness

Faithfulness follows without separation. People who are channels for the flow of peace are faithful. You can depend on them. They do what they promise. Recently I led a memorial service of thanksgiving for Senator Paul Coverdell of Georgia. He had won the trust and confidence of senators on both sides of the aisle because of his faithful service. When senators gave their eulogies, many of them choked up with tears of love and admiration for the senator. No one in the Senate worked harder or longer hours or with greater dedication than Senator Coverdell. His faith made him distinguished for his faithfulness. He spelled love: _l-o-y-a-l-t-y._

Gentleness

Authentic gentleness is one of the most miraculous manifestations of the inner power that comes from Christ's indwelling. In fact, there is no other way to be gentle than by the power the Lord gives us. It requires absolute trust in His ongoing work in others. It responds to the wonder of what people have been through, not what they have done. It addresses the emerging child, often hurt and battered, in other people.

The Lord is consistently gentle with us. He stands beside us in the midst of trouble and tragedy, nursing us through it all. This is the same kind of encouragement the people around us need.

What does it mean to be gentle in life's tensions and problems? It certainly does not mean having a moldable, adjustable, easy lack of concern. Moses was described as one of the meekest men in all of Israel, and yet he marshaled the mass exodus of a diverse company of people and brought them through the wilderness to the promised land.

Lording it over others is a sure sign we need the Lord. When we are truly meek, we know who we are because we know to whom we belong. We do not have to be defensive or justify ourselves any longer. We know we are loved and are therefore free to love and free to be the unique, special, unreproducible wonders that God meant us to be. Defensive pride is taken from us by an authentic experience of humility; we are able to treat others like God treats us. Only a person who is unsure of himself and of Christ is afraid to be gentle.

Self-Control

The Greek word for *self-control, enkrateia,* is rooted in *kratos,* which means "to have strength to control what we say and do and how we act and react." When we have peace at the center of our lives, we have no need to speak egregiously or act eccentrically.

Self-control as a fruit of the Spirit gives us the operative peace of allowing the Spirit to control how we use our aptitudes and how we satisfy our appetites. We can have power over ourselves only when we have submitted to the Spirit's control and power over us. This gives us not only deep peace but inner control and direction.

The Miraculous Growth of the Fruit

The image of fruit primarily is concerned with the process of growth. Whether a seed is immersed in the soil, in the soft, silent womb, or deep in the human spirit, all new births are intricately programmed for growth. Once we commit our lives to Christ and invite the seed of His Spirit to live in us, the miraculous growth process of the fruit of the Spirit begins and never ends.

Over the years I've learned simply to accept the mystery of how the fruit of the Spirit grows in us. All I know is that daily prayer for the fruit to be manifested in my character has been answered in wonderful ways that have given me the peace that results from love and joy. I'm amazed by the ability to express that peace in my relationships and responsibilities. Try it yourself. It works!

The old Gaelic saying is true, "Belong to God, become a wonder to yourself and a joy to your friends!"

PRAYER FOR THE FRUIT OF THE SPIRIT

Lord Christ, You are the true vine. I pray that I may abide in You today. I commit my life and professional plans to You and trust You with complete control over my life. Let me rest my insufficiencies in Your all-sufficient hands. Dear Lord, plant Your Spirit in me so that I may feel the peace that comes with the unbroken connection to Your love, joy, kindness, goodness, faithfulness, and gentleness. Thank You in advance for the chance to belong to You, to become a wonder to myself, and to become a joy to my friends. Amen.

Chapter 10

THE PEACE OF ABUNDANT RESOURCES

Therefore be merciful, just as your Father also is merciful. Judge not, and you shall not be judged. Condemn not, and you shall not be condemned. Forgive, and you will be forgiven. Give, and it will be given to you: good measure, pressed down, shaken together, and running over will be put into your bosom. For with the same measure that you use, it will be measured back to you.
—LUKE 6:36-38

A few years ago, I was on an airline going from Minneapolis to Sioux City, Iowa. The pilot announced that our flight attendant's name was Jennifer. It was a little plane, and Jennifer had the responsibility of preparing all of us so that we could have a safe flight and know exactly what we were supposed to do in case of any emergency.

What she had to say was actually very important. With airplanes going down every so often, I listened rather attentively. I looked around me, however, and no one else was listening to her as she reeled off the announcements about the fire extinguishers, the emergency doors, and what to do in case anything went wrong. She rattled it off as fast as I've ever heard anyone say it. She had memorized it from giving it so often. Her words flowed in rapid-fire order.

And then she walked past me and said, "Well, how'd I do?" I said, "I didn't understand a word you said." And she said, "You know, familiarity really makes things dull. I've done that five times today, and I've done it hundreds of times recently. I'm tired of it. Nobody listens anyhow."

It reminded me of a flight that I took some years ago in New England. The flight attendant was celebrating a very special day in her life. She was going to get married and to each person who went by, she said, "This is a wonderful day. I'm going to get married." No one responded. Can you imagine that? That lovely young woman was just bursting with enthusiasm, and these grim professionals walked by her and didn't even hear what she said.

Well, she got on the intercom system and gave all the appropriate announcements. Then at the end of it she said, "After we take off, we're going to fly to Cuba, and you all are going to be incarcerated for the rest of your lives." I looked around me, and nobody was paying attention. Can you imagine? All of the passengers stayed impassive. Not one of them put down his or her paper and said, "What did she say?"

Just like those passengers, there are times when we take God so much for granted that we ignore some of His quite amazing, startling, and awesome promises. We react as if it were all just ho-hum stuff.

Amazing Promises

Did you ever focus on the fact that each day God promises to do wonders for you that He has never done before? We've learned that God's peace gives us confidence to face whatever life dishes out. There can be no peace until we're sure that the Lord will provide what we will need. But the amazing message of the Bible is that He not only promises to meet our needs, He promises to go to the limits and then go way beyond. And so we can adopt the psalmist's positive attitude: "But I will hope continually, and will praise You yet more and more. My mouth shall tell of Your righteousness and Your salvation all the day, for I do not know their limits. I will go in the strength of the Lord GOD" (Psalm 71:14-16).

It is God's way to always go beyond the best that He has done before. As a result, a living faith will always have in it a dynamic element of surprise, tension, and discovery. What we have seen and learned up to now will not be the end of our growth or the sum total of our learning. Whatever we have found in Christ up to now is only a fraction of what we will be able to find. The Lord is not finished with us. We are a work in process. Deep peace settles in our souls when we realize that He has taken charge of our personality formation. "We are His workmanship" (Ephesians 2:10).

Peace comes from the calm conviction that whatever we've learned up to now barely scratches the surface of what we will discover. Our relationship with Christ is only the beginning of what we will experience in companionship with Him; His character has only begun to be manifested in us; His strength for life's challenges has only slightly been tested; His guidance has hardly been tapped. The fruit and gifts of the Spirit, as discussed in the previous chapter, have not been experienced and found wanting; they simply have not been experienced fully.

The Holy Spirit has not exhausted His energies and fallen into abeyance; He is ready at any moment to burst out anew and take control. In William Carey's words, now is a time "to expect great things from God and to attempt great things for God."

Expanding Returns

This stirring conviction of inexhaustible supply is based on one of Jesus' most salient statements, one of the most awesome things God said to Him, and some of the most dynamic assertions about Jesus stated by the early church. What Christ said, what God said to Him, and what the authors of the epistles in the New Testament said about Jesus give us the basis of what I'd like to call the law of expanding returns.

In the eighteenth century, an economist by the name of Turgot established what he called the law of diminishing returns. Stated simply, he reasoned that an overinvestment of capital or labor results in a diminished profit.

For example, a business needs a certain amount of capital for raw materials, facilities, and labor to produce, package, and distribute a product. Once a selling price is established in the competitive market, any additional, unnecessary, or excessive investment for production eventually lessens the profit. The overinvestment really becomes counterproductive to the ultimate purpose of making a profit.

Seventeen centuries before Turgot, Jesus proclaimed a vital truth which could be called the law of expanding returns. We find the basis for this law in Luke's account of the Sermon on the Mount where Christ says,

> Therefore be merciful, just as your Father also is merciful. Judge not, and you shall not be judged. Con-

demn not, and you shall not be condemned. Forgive, and you will be forgiven. Give, and it will be given to you: good measure, pressed down, shaken together, and running over will be put into your bosom. For with the same measure that you use, it will be measured back to you.

—LUKE 6:36-38

From this we see that we are called into partnership with the Lord to live merciful, nonjudgmental, noncondemnatory, giving, and forgiving lives. That's the product. And to produce that through us, the Lord lavishes us with an overabundance of His grace because He wants us to emulate His own generous heart.

A Plentiful Harvest

Now, I'm going to use a bit of "sanctified imagination" and suggest what I think might have been in Jesus' mind when He used this generosity metaphor. This is the picture I see. The Palestinian sun is setting over a field that has just been harvested by the combined efforts of a landowner and his laborers.

Tired, sweaty, and weary after days of harvesting grain, the servants gather around the master to receive their pay for the hard labor of planting, cultivating, and harvesting the wheat. Months before, they had held bushel baskets for the master to fill with seed for the planting. Now they hold the same measures to be filled with the harvested and threshed grain. An equal measure is the due reward for their efforts.

The servants are wearing long, loose-fitting, sheath-like garments made of coarse material which extend down to their feet. Ropelike girdles or belts are tied around their waists. But now we see that each servant has pulled up the material above the belt and formed a large pocket on his chest. Since there are no other pockets in the laborer's garb, this newly formed pocket above the waist is especially important. Each servant arranges his pocket to make it as large as possible.

The air is festive with the celebration of the harvest. They have all worked hard. Master and servants are now friends because of their labor together. Now they can enjoy the results of their work. And the master knows that his servants are deserving of their wages.

Thankful for the bountiful harvest, the master lifts sack after sack of grain and fills his servants' bushel baskets to the top. But when that is done, he still wants them to have more. So he pours more grain into their baskets until they overflow.

"Ah, that's still not enough!" the master says, his voice filled with laughter. Now he presses down the grain in the baskets to make room for more. It is a treasured moment of mutual affirmation. Now the master lifts all of the bushels, shaking them vigorously to make more room for still more grain. On top of the compacted grain, he pours more. Again it spills over on the ground.

Even with that, the master's generosity has not found sufficient expression. Now he notices the empty pockets formed on the servants' chests from the folds of their robes. And with a twinkle in his eye, he begins filling the pockets full as well. The servants, sensing the master's joy, join in the merriment and pull more of the material of their garments above their girdles to provide even bigger pockets which the master immediately fills to overflowing.

And then in a final expression of shared celebration, the master takes handfuls of grain and showers the servants with it, tossing some in their hair and pouring still more down the backs of their necks.

Everyone feels a great sense of joy and satisfaction. Their job is finished for now, but it won't be long before the servants will work for the master again on the next project. They are important to his strategy, and they are dependent on his provision.

I'm convinced that something like that drama is suggested by Jesus' metaphor. The words _running over will be put into your bosom_ prompted my thought about what might have been the basis of His impelling word-picture. The word _bosom_, which in some translations is rendered _heart_, is _kolpos_ in the Greek text. It really means "pocket." Since there were no pockets in laborers' garments worn in the field, I agree with many interpreters that what is meant is the pocket formed above the waist that I've described.

What I think Jesus means by this metaphor is not only an equal or even pressed-down, overflowing bushel basket, but in addition a filled-up, spilling-over pocket. That's the way God is with us. He wants us to overflow with His peace. The more we use what He invests in us, the more peace He desires to give us.

Steps to Receiving Overflowing Peace

This limitless peace of Christ will be given to us when we follow Jesus' action steps. Let's reflect further on the implied progression of His metaphor, "Give and it will be given to you." Give what? Note what precedes this admonition.

"Therefore be merciful, just as your Father also is merciful. Judge not, and you shall not be judged. Condemn not, and you shall not be condemned. Forgive, and you will be forgiven" (Luke 6:36-37). All these are action steps in the application of generous love about which Jesus has been teaching in the passage. Now the metaphor becomes vividly clear. When we reproduce that quality of love in our relationships and responsibilities, we are not only replenished in equal but in overflowing measure. Having followed Jesus' fivefold action steps, we are ready to claim an overflowing outpouring of His peace.

Two stages of blessing are implied. First comes recognition of how much we have received of the Lord's provision, His providential care, love, and forgiveness through the cross. That prompts us to respond in faith with the commitment of our lives. A new life in Christ begins. But it's when we begin to share what we have received that we discover the secret of infilling power. Then we realize that the overflowing grain of Jesus' metaphor is really His own Spirit. And there's no limit to how much He wants to give us of Himself.

Generosity

What would you say is the distinguishing quality of a truly dynamic Christian? Great faith, sound convictions, impeccable character? No, I think it's generosity: the freedom to give and receive unqualified, nonmanipulative love. And for that we must discover how to receive graciously. What the Lord wants from us, He gives to us in abundance. This is what I believe Jesus is saying in this metaphor of generosity. We need generosity to combat one of our greatest problems—that of selfishness.

Now I want you to pay careful attention as I share with you a paradox, and it's a paradox with which we must come to grips. Point number one: God owns everything. He is Lord of all. "The earth is the Lord's and the fullness thereof; the world, and all of those who dwell therein," said the psalmist. True? Would you say that God owns everything?

All right. Now the other half of the paradox. What doesn't God have—unless it's given to Him? Your heart.

I know people who are in power struggles with God. Then there are those who are struggling to gain His power for their own purposes. Both of these are losers. The winners are those who surrender their control to the Lord's control. Only as we do that can we participate in the law of expanding returns.

The Problem of Selfishness

Many people have told me that they believe selfishness is the number one problem facing us today. But most of the time we don't see it as our problem; we think it applies to *other* people.

And yet selfishness, the inordinate concern for ourselves, is a problem we all face at times—some people, most of the time. Growing out of an inadequate experience of grace, we fear that there won't be enough of life's blessings to go around. So we measure everything in terms of what's happening to us, what we get, and what we need for our sense of security and satisfaction. Our concerns are whether we get what is coming to us and whether or not people are paying attention to us. Selfishness is not self-love; it's an aching need to experience the Lord's gracious love for us.

In our selfishness we get caught up in a power struggle to try to gain and keep control over ourselves, others, and even God. We become defensive of our turf and want to impress our wills on other people. We want what we want when we want it.

Some time ago, a friend of mine called me long-distance to share his disappointment over being bypassed for a key position as head of his department in a large Midwest corporation. After the shock of not receiving the promotion he'd been working for all these years, he sublimated his anger with a determination to keep control of the department even though someone else would be in charge.

"It doesn't make any difference who's in charge, just so I'm still in control!" my friend said.

"Sounds like you're heading for a no-win power struggle," I cautioned.

"Maybe so," my friend responded, "but no one knows this department better than I do, and I'm not about to lose all the effort and hard work I've put into building it up over the years. I don't really care who has the title—just so I still can call the shots."

My friend's lust for selfish control was not really surprising. I hear the same battle for power in husbands and wives who are in deadly struggles for selfish control. Parents express it about children who threaten their control. People feel it about friends who dare to resist their forceful manipulations. Churches and movements are often rendered ineffective by individuals and groups seeking to selfishly dominate.

The lust for control is not just the problem of the more obvious power brokers. It's in all of us. Our struggles for selfish control eventually block the flow of power from the Lord. But He is able to bless those who put their lives under His control.

Reluctant Receivers

One of the great causes of selfishness is the difficulty we have receiving the blessings the Lord offers us. We are reluctant receivers! But He doesn't give up.

How does the Lord deal with selfishness? Does He take away what we have to shock us awake to our self-centered attitudes? Sometimes. But most often He employs the law of expanding returns. He knows our problems stem from not knowing how to give ourselves away generously. And so He melts our icy hearts with the warmth of His goodness rather than smashing us with condemnatory judgments. Often He uses the very problems we experience to show us His faithfulness, and His consistent interventions finally convince us of the limitless generosity in His heart.

The Lord knows He finally has gotten through to us when we come to the place of wanting to be as generous with others as He has been to us. But in order to do that we need power. And that's exactly what the Lord offers to provide.

Power for Our
Real Purpose

The Lord's power is given for the accomplishment of His purposes. That's the secret of receiving unlimited peace. He wants to make us like Himself.

What God demands from us, He develops in us; what He requires, He releases in bountiful measure; what He decides, He provides. Our God is our eternal, sovereign, and enabling savior, challenging father, and comforting friend. We are never left to try and make it on our own. And no matter how much we give, we can't outgive the Lord. Our Lord can't give enough to those who seek to emulate His character of mercy without condemnatory judgment and with giving, forgiving love. When we meet His qualifications, there's no restriction on how much peace He's willing to give us. The law is simple: Give and it will be given to you. Start today!

PRAYER FOR OVERFLOWING PEACE

Generous Lord, thank You for Your amazing promises! You have offered me the abounding, unsearchable riches of Your limitless resources. There are no restrictions on how much You will give! And what can I give in response? Help me to know what You want from me so that I may be unlimited in my service to You. May this be a day when I have the power to accomplish Your purposes in all of my responsibilities and relationships. I praise You for the opportunity to toil in Your fields, surrounded by Your plentiful harvest of overflowing peace. Amen.

Chapter 11

DON'T HOLD YOUR PEACE

Blessed are the peacemakers, for they shall be called sons of God.
—MATTHEW 5:9

A recent debate over issues on the Senate floor escalated into an acrimonious shouting match between a Republican and a Democrat. I went to both men to listen to their complaints and pray with them that the Lord would show them how to compromise creatively and do what would be best for our nation. Later that evening, both men prayed about what they should do. The next day, communication was reestablished, and the Senate went forward with the day's business.

When I prayed at the opening of that day's session, I did not take sides but called for all the senators and all of us who work with them to be sure we were on God's side rather than trying to get Him on our side. I share that prayer with you here because it may be applicable to relationships and situations where you are called to be a peacemaker.

Spirit of the living God, fall afresh on this Senate chamber. Enter the mind and heart of each senator and reign as Sovereign over all that is said and done this day. We confess that it is sometimes easier to use pious words to pray about Your presence and power than it is to turn over the control of our lives and our work to You. We are all strong-willed people; we want things done our way, and often we are better at manipulation than mediation. Built right into our two-party system is the potential for discord and the lack of civility. It's so easy for all of us, senators and staff, to get suited up like mountain climbers and scramble over molehills. Procedures can become more important than progress and winning more crucial than being willing to work together. Make us party to Your plans for America rather than planning only for our party.

Now at the beginning of this day, remind the senators and all of us who serve with them that this is Your Senate, that we are accountable to You, and that we could not breathe our next breath without Your permission. Keep our attention on what needs to be done now rather than on how what is said and done will impact a future election. In our minds' eye we picture a day in which we can put You and our nation first. We humble ourselves least we be humiliated by missing Your call to greatness. In the name of the Prince of Peace. Amen.

You can imagine that this prayer initiated some good conversations with senators on both sides of the aisle. But peacemaking in the political arena is never a done deal. Each day brings new opportunities to help senators and their staffs discover that debate is meant to expose deeper truths on both sides of an issue that will lead to a more refined piece of legislation. What's important is what is best for America; getting leaders to seek God's will and then to listen to one another is the never-ending challenge.

As chaplain of the Senate, one of my most challenging responsibilities is as a peacemaker. This demanding task has forced me to rediscover in a practical way what Jesus meant when He called peacemakers not only blessed, but sons and daughters of God our Father, called into the family business of peacemaking.

The Call to Peacemaking

Peacemaking is an obvious part of my present position. It is no less your responsibility. To be in Christ is to be in peacemaking. In this chapter of our ongoing conversation about perfect peace, I'd like to share with you some of what the Lord is teaching me about being a peacemaker. The title of this chapter is a play on the phrase, "Don't hold your peace." Usually *holding our peace* means "remaining silent, not saying what we really think, or avoiding conflict." What I want to communicate here is that our peace needs to be given away, shared with others so that it becomes the basis of reconciliation between people and groups.

We covered the need to forgive in chapter 5. Peacemaking expands that concept. Allow me to ask you some questions that will focus on your own personal evaluation of your need to let go of your peace.

Is there anyone in your life who urgently needs peace right now? Do you have a broken relationship that needs mending? Do you know of any people who are at odds with each other? Do you long to bring them some semblance of peaceful relationship and communication? Do you know what to say, what to do?

Do you know of any groups who are facing hostility and anxiousness with each other because of differences? We all know people separated on political issues, ideologies, and approaches to government. Are you also aware of people who are separated because of racial differences, dissimilar cultural backgrounds, opposing creedal beliefs, differing status in society? Do you long to bring peace into these situations? If you know about any of these problems, would you like to know what to do to help the people involved?

Steps to Becoming a Peacemaker

The first step to becoming a peacemaker is to accept your calling. Each of us has been called to be a priest of peace. We are all part of the priesthood of believers with God's mandate in our souls to bring peace to other people. The priesthood of all believers is solidly rooted in the Scriptures. Peter called us "a chosen generation, a royal priesthood, a holy nation, His own special people, that you may proclaim the praises of Him who called you out of darkness into His marvelous light" (1 Peter 2:9).

Have you ever thought of yourself as a priest? Did you wake up this morning and say, "Lord, bless my priesthood today"?

A priest is one who goes to God on behalf of other people and then brings the blessings of God to them. A priest also serves as a bridge over the gap between God and people or between one person and another. A priest is also a mediator, one who declares truth and brings healing.

Every Christian has the right to pray directly to God and receive His blessing. But that's only half of it. Every believer is also called to minister in a priesthood to other people. When we are in Christ we are in the priesthood, in the ministry with a calling to intercede on behalf of other people and then bring the peace of Jesus Christ to them. We can't escape. We can't be _in_ Christ and _out_ of the priesthood of peacemaking. The question isn't whether you're a priest or not. The real question is what kind you are and to what extent you're being effective in your peace priesthood. It's a part of your rebirth right. And what a privilege! Jesus said, "Blessed are the peacemakers, for they shall be called sons of God" (Matthew 5:9). You and I are daughters and sons of God, and we're blessed because we have the calling to be peacemakers—to be involved in bringing peace to people, to groups, and to our communities. We are meant to be reconcilers in the midst of brokenness and hostility.

A Garland of Greatness

"Blessed are the peacemakers, for they shall be called sons of God" (Matthew 5:9).

I believe that this beatitude is the clasp on the garland of greatness of all nine of the beatitudes. But the ones that go before it describe the qualities that make it possible for us to be peacemakers. Reviewing them is excellent preparation for the ministry of peacemaking.

"Blessed are the poor in spirit, for theirs is the kingdom of heaven" (Matthew 5:3).

The truly happy, the blessed, are the poor in spirit. We can't be peacemakers if we haven't first been poor in spirit, known spiritual poverty, and cried out to God for help. No arrogant person is ever able to bring peace to anyone else. Humility is the key. All that we have and are is the result of God's love and care. When we've known poverty of spirit and cried out for God's love and forgiveness and have received His grace, we have taken the first step in preparing to be peacemakers.

"Blessed are those who mourn, for they shall be comforted" (Matthew 5:4).

There are no worthy peacemakers I know who haven't known profound mourning over their own sins and failures, the corporate sins of the church, the falling of creation, the degradation of society. Out of that pain comes the ability to identify with other people's pain and the ability to communicate peace that's real, that's been tested, that's been ground out in the crucible of experience. After the hot tears of repentance have flowed, we're able to approach people honestly, with freedom and profound love. This is an absolutely necessary part of the preparation for becoming a peacemaker.

"Blessed are the meek, for they shall inherit the earth" (Matthew 5:5).

Peacemakers also have known the meekness of coming under the leading and power of the Spirit. Meekness isn't mealymouthed adjustability; it's the ability to allow God to guide us. Peacemakers are those who are no longer running their own lives. Peacemakers who are meek, who are led by the Lord, are effective and powerful. They also live under the plumb line of the righteousness of God. They know what's wrong because they've read the Bible and have a sense of the urgent needs of people and society. God's plumb line has come down on their own lives, and they're no longer judgmental and negative about other people. They can go to others with love because they have felt the fire of God's judgment in their own lives—and, as a consequence, have received His grace! That's what's required to be a peacemaker.

"Blessed are those who hunger and thirst for righteousness, for they shall be filled" (Matthew 5:6).

In the fourth beatitude, Jesus declares that the blessed desire righteousness more than a starving person longs for food or a parched person for water. Peacemakers must seek God's righteousness with a consuming passion. They must long for other people to experience a right relationship with God through Christ and seek His righteousness in all of life.

The questions to ask when trying to mend broken relationships and strife are, "What does God want?" and "What is His best for all concerned?" Peace results from being right with God. Often our task is to help people sort out what may be keeping them from God's perfect peace. When a person experiences a new relationship with God, he or she will be much more open to reconciliation with others. Wonderful relationships can begin to develop.

"Blessed are the merciful, for they shall obtain mercy" (Matthew 5:7).

Now consider how the merciful make good peacemakers. To be merciful is to get inside of another person's skin and feel what he or she is feeling. An aspect of the meaning of the Hebrew word for *mercy* is "the attentive love and care for an unborn child who can do nothing to earn his status or care." Mercy is feeling with other people what they're feeling. It's their pain in your heart. In Christ, God has broken the cycle of judgment and retaliation. We have received mercy—undeserved and unearned love. In the fifth beatitude, Jesus invites us to share His character trait of mercy. But inflow and outgo must be matched. Mercy must be given away if we want to live in its flow.

The test of the greatness Christ offers us is to be merciful to those who do not "deserve" it or return it. When we've endured disappointment, injustice, or hurt, we must not become bitter; we must draw on and express mercy. This is not easy—not until we remember how merciful Christ has been to us. We are called to be channels of divine mercy, letting it flow through us to others. This is our source of strength as peacemakers.

"Blessed are the pure in heart, for they shall see God" (Matthew 5:8).

Next, Christ gives us a prescription for both seeing things close at hand and seeing at a distance. Our hearts have eyes. They are our "inner eyes" with which we see God and discern His will for the future. But our hearts' eyes are often impaired because of the spiritual cataracts of willfulness and secondary loyalties. Kierkegaard said, "Purity of heart is to will one thing." A heart that is able to see God is one in which there are no conflicting loyalties or hidden sin to cloud the vision. Purity is singleness of focused vision.

How do we purify our hearts? After reviewing the six-way test for peace-guided thinking on pages 99-100, clean your heart out with confession. What are you holding in your heart that contradicts your commitment to the Lord? Resentments? Jealousies? Unconfessed sin? Fantasies? Plans our Lord could not bless? The second step is to invite the Holy Spirit into your heart. He is like a lens implant that clears your vision, enabling you to see God, discern His will, and see at a distance what He wants you to do. Just as the fluid in the physical eye keeps it cleansed, so the Holy Spirit cleanses, dilates, and focuses the vision of the spiritual eyes of the heart.

Peacemaking—the Family Business

Now we can appreciate our awesome calling to be peacemakers. All of the above attributes are required to go into our Father's business.

In our relationship with the heavenly Father, we express our family likeness by manifesting the fruit of the Spirit of peace and by doing what's important to Him: peacemaking. Jesus said, "I must be about My Father's business" (Luke 2:49). He came to bring peace, made peace through the blood of the cross, and called us to be peacemakers. Peacemaking is the family business we all share. Daily we receive a fresh experience of His last will and testament: "Peace I leave with you, My peace I give to you."

When peace resides in our hearts we can be peacemakers. We can become the initial reconcilers of conflict. Our part of the family business consists of tearing down walls and constantly working for understanding. We live in a world where people and groups are at enmity. We are called to constantly and actively seek to resolve these conflicts. We must listen to, love, and care for people on both sides without taking sides, for we stand on the side of peace.

Peacemaking Begins with Ourselves

Peacemaking begins with a profound experience of peace. But we can't give away something we don't have. We can't be peacemakers unless peace is the pervading quality of our lives. Let me suggest that peace must begin by peacemaking with ourselves before we can go on to share it with anyone else.

Sometimes I'm my worst judge. You should hear the tongue-lashing I give myself at the end of some days. "Lloyd, how could you have said that? Why did you do that? Why didn't you do something else?" Do you ever say that to yourself?

Consistent peace that overflows to other people comes from an inner peace that is an expression of daring to love that never-to-be-repeated miracle that is you. This isn't self-adulation. It's an affirmation that comes out of God's powerful grace and forgiveness. It's a terrible thing to spend your life being down on yourself. Peace comes when we dare to make peace with that aggressive, competitive, dissatisfied, longing, rebellious person inside. Paul did that. His experience of the grace of God finally got into the depths of his being and healed the person he had become. Once he made peace with himself, he could become an effective peacemaker with other people.

Initiating Peace

So often when I talk with people about strained or broken relationships they exclaim, "Hey, wait a minute. I'm not to blame. The other person hurt me. Let him or her come to me. Don't tell me I've got to go to them." That's the way most of us feel, and that's why there's so little reconciliation that takes place. Everybody's waiting around, waiting for the other person to make the first move with an apology.

Being a peacemaker means being an initiator in relationships where there is brokenness. Every one of us has relationships that are filled with hurt, pain, and distress through misunderstandings. It's a terrible thing to feel misjudged and to be misinterpreted. And it's disturbing to feel the hurt and pain of rejection. Who hasn't had a share of this kind of suffering? But to be a peacemaker is to be the initiator, the one who goes first to bring healing.

A peacemaker senses the great need in other people. The deepest need is for God Himself, to be filled with His peace, to be at peace, and then to be able to share with other people what that peace really means.

To Whom Do You Report?

The Lord is the only one we have to please. When you consider that, you have nothing to lose. We know that He will guide us and provide us the inspiration and direction that we need. So we can be the ones who take the first step, whether another person does or not.

Is there anyone you need to call or write to ask for forgiveness? To extend forgiveness? To make amends or restitution? Anyone in your life? Why wait? You may not have another chance. Do it now. Do it today. Remember the sad story of Bates and Drummond!

Being a Reconciler

As I mentioned, a peacemaker is also someone who is aware of the discord and disharmony between other people. When people come to us to tell us what someone has said or done to them, our calling as a peacemaker is to say, "I know how you're feeling, and I understand why you've reacted the way you have. But there's not going to be any healing until you talk to the person you're angry with. I want to help you get together with him or her. Would you like me to be there? Come, let's go tell that person what you've just told me."

Sometimes we do just the opposite. We listen to a person tell us about someone else, smack our lips and say, "Really? Tell me more!" Sometimes we add to the criticism, and a little spark bursts into a big bonfire. It isn't long before we've joined in committing character assassination. At the very time when we could be of help, we've added to the hurt.

Peacemakers must give up the sinful luxury of gossip. For some people, that's harder than giving up smoking cigarettes or drinking too much alcohol. It's an addiction. And any addiction, including gossip, substitutes for something that we really should seek from God. At its worst it is a virulent gossip that destroys. The Spanish proverb is right: "If people gossip *to* you, be sure of this: They will gossip *about* you."

A peacemaker is one who builds up trust because others know that whatever is said will never be repeated. A peacemaker gives up the temptation to titillate his or her own ego with condemnatory analysis of other people.

One of the hardest decisions I ever made, which I have to resolve to again and again, I made years ago in my ministry. I decided that I would never say anything about another person that I hadn't first said to that person or was willing to say within a 24-hour period. That is the toughest decision for leadership I've ever made. Sometimes I fail, but it sure does cut the taproot of gossip!

A peacemaker is one who feels deeply the yearning of God to bring reconciliation between people who are estranged. We stand in the gap with two hands—one to grasp one person and the other to grasp the other person—then with both arms, we draw them together. We care for and encourage them until all of the things that are hurting and causing pain are out in the open and can be healed by the grace of God.

Peacemakers allow the plumb line of Jesus Christ's justice to fall on the communities of which they are a part. Anything that robs people of the ability to discover or grow in peace becomes the focus of our calling as priests of peace. We are called to become active whenever we can bring healing and hope.

As Chaplain of the Senate, I've come to know most of the senators on a personal basis. Senator Bill Frist of Tennessee comes to mind as one who has answered the call of peacemaker—not only in the Senate, but in faraway lands where war has raged for decades.

A noted physician and surgeon, Frist has earned the respect of senators on both sides of the aisle, partly because he always seems to be on call—to talk, to listen, and to bring people together. Perhaps it is his medical training and years as a physician that have caused him to accept this role as healer—that have made him willing to bridge the gap between opposing camps. But more likely it is his own faith in Jesus Christ that enables him to reach out to others with needs greater than his own. But the peace he gives away is not limited to Washington. Each year he travels to sub-Saharan Africa with the missionary organization Samaritan's Purse, bringing not just his surgical skills and services, but also food, medicine, and most importantly, the truth about Jesus Christ. Their motto is "We treat; Jesus heals."

Are you a peacemaker or a peace-breaker? Are you a peacemaker or troublemaker? Do you enable peace or do you spread discord? What kind of person are you...am I? The blessed, the truly happy, the irrepressibly joyous people are those who have made commitments to be priests of peace. And the reward? To be the "daughters and sons of God," which is the Hebrew way of saying "being like God." Not a bad offer for the likes of you and me!

Five Fingers of Peace

Last December I was invited to Belfast in Northern Ireland to speak at a series of Christmas peace celebrations. Thirteen hundred people packed the Waterfront Conference Center for each of the four celebrations of music and messages of peace. At that time Northern Ireland was enjoying an uneasy respite in the conflict between the Roman Catholics and the Protestants. A new government had been formed, and the future looked hopeful. People from the various sides of the conflict attended the Christmas peace celebrations, some of them seated next to each other. Old hatreds and animosities had been set aside in the name of the Prince of Peace and in the ambience of the continued negotiations.

One of the most moving parts of the celebration was a performance by a high school choir made up of young people from Protestant and Roman Catholic schools in Portadown, one of the places of the most fierce and bloody conflict. The young men and women exemplified the hope for a united, peaceful Northern Ireland. They were determined to sing together. "The shooting, killing, and hatred have to stop. We want peace!" one student exclaimed to me.

My message each evening was entitled "The Five Fingers of Peace." I shared the meaning of reaching out with the five fingers of our hands to give peace to each other. I talked about the five aspects of true peace: a Christ-filled heart, a loving heart, a forgiving heart, a peacemaking heart, and a peace-guarded-and-guided heart.

At the conclusion of each of the services I asked the people to turn and give the sign of peace to each other. That was not easy for those seated beside old enemies or people who had been responsible for the death of a father, son, or brother. And yet, most people flexed the five fingers of peace, remembering what each one meant and grasped the hand of the person on the right, left, in front, and behind. One man told me later how traumatic the experience had been. "I had to give the peace to a man who had shot my son. It wasn't easy but I did it in Jesus' name. Only He could have given me the courage to do it!" the man said with a quivering voice and tears in his eyes.

Sometimes peacemaking isn't easy; in fact, sometimes it's almost impossible. And there are times when it doesn't seem to make any lasting difference. At this writing, just six months after being in Belfast for the peace conference, violence has broken out again. But I keep remembering those high school students in that choir who modeled Christ's peace. They are our hope for a new generation of peace-loving people. The future of Northern Ireland is theirs. They have and will make the lasting difference. They are true peacemakers working in their heavenly Father's business. You can be too!

PRAYER FOR BECOMING
A PEACEMAKER

Father, I commit myself to be a peacemaker. I confess that it is so easy to sow discord, fan fires of misunderstanding between people, and take sides in conflicts. I ask for the gift of peace so I can experience and express Christ's serenity, tranquillity, and reconciliation. Help me be quick to forgive, slow to judge, and resourceful when people are at odds with each other. I want to be a reconciler who brings estranged people and groups together. I can't produce peace but I can propagate the peace that already has been given to me through the blood of Christ on the cross. I want every person to possess that kind of peace to heal their broken and strained relationships. I want every compound fracture between groups to be reset by it, for all misunderstandings and hatred to be liberated by it. You have told me that the only way to be happy and truly blessed is to become involved in peacemaking. Thank You for offering me a partnership in Your family business. Amen.

Chapter 12

A GOAL FOR TODAY BIG ENOUGH FOR ETERNITY

I have fought the good fight, I have finished the race,
I have kept the faith. Finally, there is laid up for me
the crown of righteousness, which the Lord, the righteous Judge,
will give to me on that Day, and not to me only
but also to all who have loved His appearing.
—2 TIMOTHY 4:7-8

The cartoon depicted a man kneeling to say his prayers. He looked up to heaven with an imploring face and said, "In the name of the Freedom of Information Act I demand to know what's in my file!"

Have you ever wanted to know what's in your eternal file? Ever wanted to ask the Lord, "How did I measure up? Am I okay? Is my life what You meant it to be? Am I really reaching Your goal for me?"

There are times in unguarded moments when we begin to feel uneasy about our lives. A loved one dies; a close friend is suffering terminal illness. A question rises out of the inner being, "What if today were my final day? Would I be ready?"

Ever wonder where you will spend eternity?

Daily Accountability

It's extremely important that we be very sure about our goals because our goal for today needs to be big enough to reach eternity. We will not have a daily experience of peace unless we can look back over each day knowing that one more day has been lived that is consistent with our eternal goal. We can know peace along the way only when we end each day with an incisive inventory of the extent to which we have accomplished our eternal goal. When we haven't, we can confess the opportunities we missed or the challenges we sidestepped and receive forgiveness. At the end of each day, Christ offers us peace for the broken promises. He promises us a new beginning for the next day. Daily accountability prepares us for our eternal accounting. And Christ wants to be sure we pass the examination with flying colors, so He helps us to know what the examination will cover.

Final Examinations

I remember three different kinds of examinations given by my professors. One teacher always put in a trick question to stump us students. We knew that obscure, esoteric question would appear somewhere in the exam. There was no way to get totally prepared. No matter how much we read or memorized, we knew that the impossible question would be there to throw us off-target and lower our grades.

Another professor didn't give any tests. There was no accountability. Each day we stumbled through the class material wondering what we were to gain from the course. Because of the lack of accountability, we didn't learn very much. At the end of the course this permissive professor would say, "Well, what kind of grade do you want?" The strange thing is that most of us students gave ourselves lower grades than he was prepared to give us.

The professor I appreciated most of all was the one who gave us the questions he was going to ask on the exam ahead of time so that we could be ready to pass with the highest grades. He wanted us to know the material. The questions encompassed what he wanted us to take away from the course. If we knew the answers to the crucial questions, he knew we were ready to graduate. I remember feeling peaceful before taking exams from that professor. I was ready!

This is exactly the way Jesus, our eternal Judge, deals with us. Each day He helps us to know what's important so when the ultimate day arrives, we are sure to pass on through to eternity. Here are his questions:

- Do you believe in Me as your Lord and Savior?

- Have you received My indwelling Spirit and accepted My character transplant that empowers you to love, serve, forgive, and care by My power?

- Are you involved in sharing with others the love and forgiveness you have received? I put a high priority on introducing others to Me. Is it your priority?

- Have you become a servant wherever you were called to pour out your life for others in practical ways?

- Are you involved in sacrificial service in areas of injustice where people suffer? Are you confronting the justice issues of your time? You can't do everything, but have you at least attempted the assignments on My agenda for you?

These are questions that determine where we will spend eternity. But they also become the questions which help us to evaluate any day as a good or bad day. We will not have peace without the assurance we've done things His way. Sometimes we must face a temporary loss of peace until we get back to what's important to Christ, who is our Judge as well as our Prince of Peace.

Paul's Survival Guide

The apostle Paul wrote to his son in the faith, Timothy, about a goal for today big enough for eternity. The apostle was at the end of his physical life, facing execution during his second imprisonment. The purpose of his letter was to teach Timothy how to survive in peace-threatening conflict, battles with heresies, divisions among believers, and the young man's constant struggle with timidity. Paul told him to stand firm, trust in Christ, and live courageously for Him.

All through Paul's letter he gives advice for fearless faithfulness. He tells Timothy, "And as for you." Then with implied "and as for me" intensity, he shares the goal that sustained him through 30 years of ministry. Paul calls Timothy to press on toward the same goal, to learn from him about how to face impossible odds in reaching that goal daily, and then to look forward to the reward from Christ, the only Judge of the performance of our lives. He clearly identified the Lord Jesus as the Judge of the living and the dead (2 Timothy 4:1).

Paul's goal for his life had been clear ever since his encounter with Christ on the Damascus road and his long period of preparation for apostleship in Arabia after his conversion. "For to me, to live is Christ" (Philippians 1:21) was Paul's purpose. His goal was equally clear:

That I may know Him and the power of His resurrection, and the fellowship of His sufferings, being conformed to His death, if, by any means, I may attain to the resurrection from the dead. Not that I have already attained, or am already perfected; but I press on, that I may lay hold of that for which Christ Jesus has also laid hold of me. Brethren, I do not count myself to have apprehended; but one thing I do, forgetting those things which are behind and reaching forward to those things which are ahead, I press toward the goal for the prize of the upward call of God in Christ Jesus.

—PHILIPPIANS 3:10-14

Paul could look back at the end of his life and see how his goal had sustained and strengthened him. He wrote to Timothy,

I have fought the good fight, I have finished the race, I have kept the faith. Finally, there is laid up for me the crown of righteousness, which the Lord, the righteous Judge, will give to me on that Day, and not to me only but also to all who have loved His appearing.

—2 TIMOTHY 4:7-8

Paul had received peace. He knew he had fought the good fight, finished the race, and kept the faith. His retrospective reflection provides us with prospective resolve to define a goal for any day that's big enough for eternity. Paul became the intentional disciple he was because his goal had been set before he began his adventuresome life as Christ's apostle, ambassador, and communicator of hope. He knew where he was going in this life and for eternity. Now he passes on to Timothy—and to us—his survival guide, the baton for our lap of the race and our source of determination to keep the faith.

True peace is maintained when we can affirm that we have lived out our eternal goal in the midst of our daily stresses. A good day ending with profound inner peace is a day in which we have fought the good fight, run the race, and kept the faith. We have a built-in alarm that blares in our souls when any day has missed all three of these. Each day is part of the cumulative days of life leading up to facing our final examination.

We are to fight the good fight.

We live our lives in spiritual warfare. The fight begins within us before we can face the good fight in the world. We fight the self-willed desire to be in control. On a daily basis we must choose to turn over to the Lord the control of that day. Our outward enemies are Satan and the people he uses. We also combat collusive evil in the structures of society that resist justice and righteousness. Along with this, we confront people's neglect, lack of caring, and mediocrity. Often the battle for faith, hope, and charity must be fought with religious people who don't know God, and yet we fight on, never giving up. But remember it's the *good* fight, not just a crusade for our personal competitive aggrandizement. The battle is the Lord's! We must keep our attention on Him and not on our own advantage. That will give freedom and peace!

We are to run the race.

Paul thought of life in Christ as a lifelong marathon that lasts as long as we are in this earthly portion of our eternal lives. And so we recommit ourselves daily to our one passion: knowing Christ, growing in His character, spreading

His love, serving in His name, and doing His will. It is interesting to note that there is no verb in the original Greek of Philippians 3:13-14, "One thing I do." It should read simply, "One thing, forgetting those things which are behind and reaching forward to those things which are ahead, I press toward the goal for the prize of the upward call of God in Christ Jesus." One thing! Peace results from doing that one thing with everything within us. A goal for today big enough for eternity!

The Greek word for _goal_ is _skopos_ from _skopeō_, "to look at." Our word _telescope_ comes from this. For Paul it meant "the mark on which he focused his eyes, his full attention." The word for _prize_ is _brabeion_, the award for finishing the race. The word is closely related to _brabeus_ (discussed in chapter 7), an umpire, one who judges the race and awards the prize. Paul's goal for his upward call of running the race of discipleship was Christ Himself. The "upward call" into heaven would be the ultimate fulfillment of the eternal life he began when he accepted Christ as Messiah, Savior, and Lord. Paul was on the way in the upward call to heaven each day of his life here on earth. There would have been no peace for Paul without this intentional daily pressing toward the goal.

We are to keep the faith.

Keeping the faith means holding on to our faith in Christ but also the composite truths of the gospel. We cannot deny truth and keep peace. The message of Christ presents us with absolutes. Our time resists dynamic absolutes. Our challenge is to live what we believe and speak the truth with love. Anytime we have a chance to communicate Christ's love and we remain silent, any situation which contradicts His call to righteousness in which we refuse to take a stand, and any time we receive clear guidance to act and we remain immobilized—we will stop up the flow of Christ's peace into our minds and hearts. Strangely enough, keeping the faith means growing in faith by giving it away.

So what's in your file? The only things that will ever be held against you are the things for which you refused to accept forgiveness or the things you refused to do even though you knew Christ called you to do them.

With Paul you can live each day knowing what is in store for you: the crown of righteousness "which the righteous Judge will give." And don't miss the secret. The crown will be given to those who have loved His appearing (2 Timothy 4:8). Now how's that for a positive perspective?

The Serendipity of God's Interventions

The Prince of Peace wants us to spend each day lovingly expecting, longing for, and wide open to our receiving His "appearances."

The other day was a great day for me because I reaffirmed that I wanted to be among those who love Christ appearing in each serendipity He produces. I started the day listing all the people for whom I was concerned. Added to that were situations in which I needed the Lord's power and presence to solve some very complicated problems. As the day went on, one surprise of grace followed another.

I knew that a certain senator was facing a serious family problem. I prayed asking that I would be given an opportunity to talk with him. As it turned out, I ran into him coming out of the Senate chamber. We found a quiet place to talk and pray. What could have taken days to arrange, the Lord pulled off within an hour of my prayer.

An hour later another senator came up to me on the side of the chamber where I was standing. "Pray for me," he said. "I've got a tough speech coming up."

Still another senator reported on an experiment in praise and thanksgiving we'd committed to do together. He had felt a lack of peace in his life, and I had shared with him the Scriptures in which we are called to rejoice in tough times. "It works, Chaplain!" he exclaimed. "I've made it through the past few days at peace and I'm filled with inspiration. The tougher things got, the more I thanked the Lord for the privilege."

At noon I taught the Senators' Bible Study. I sensed an obvious openness, an eagerness to claim Christ's promise to turn wearisome worry into creative concern. The prayer time was powerful. Christ was there! And we were present in the present moment to receive His presence.

The rest of the day flowed with equal delight. Counseling, phone calls to people in the hospital, an opportunity to communicate grace to a discouraged television broadcaster, and a time of prayer with a custodian. And that's only a portion of what the Lord did in His "appearing."

When You Reach a Spiritual Impasse

There's a spiritual truth we must face. If our quest for Christ's peace continues only to be for ourselves and our personal comfort, we will reach the stage where our faith becomes stagnant and we no longer sense His power and presence. The reason is quite simple: We are called to be communicators of Christ's peace. Sure signs that we are denying the calling: a plateau of spiritual growth or a time when we sense the absence of Christ's presence. The opposite is Paul's conviction: "But the Lord stood with me and strengthened me" (2 Timothy 4:17).

Peace at the End of the Race

If we come to the end of each day asking, "Have I fought the good fight? Have I run the race? Have I kept the faith?" then in a marvelous way, day by day, our files are cleared, and we can be sure if this were our last day, we'd graduate to heaven. If we really want true peace we have to be sure where we will spend eternity. Fear of death cancels our sense of peace.

So what's in your file? You don't need to appeal in the name of the Freedom of Information Act. Christ will tell you whatever is lacking. He's on your side, not against you. And He wants you to live fully now and forever with His perfect peace!

PRAYER FOR ETERNAL LIFE

Eternal God, thank You for offering me Your perfect peace for this day. Be with me as I fight the good fight, finish the race, and keep the faith. Help me to commit this day to becoming prepared for the final accounting. Thank You for giving me the peace of knowing that I will be alive forever and that I will spend eternity in the full realization of the joy of life with You. In the name of Jesus who died to give me eternal life. Amen.

QUOTE BIBLIOGRAPHY

Chapter 2, p. 14
Alec J. Motyer, *Isaiah: an Introduction and Commentary* (Downers Grove, IL: Inter-Varsity Press, 1999), pp. 174-75.

Chapter 2, p. 15
J.N. Oswalt, *The Book of Isaiah* (Grand Rapids, MI: Wm. B. Eerdmans Publishing Co., 1986), p. 468.

Chapter 3, p. 24
H. G. Wells, *The Outline of History* (New York: The Macmillan Company, 1921), p. 594.

Chapter 3, p. 32
Charles Norman, *e. e. cummings: The Magic-Maker* (New York: The Bobbs-Merrill Company, Inc., 1972), p. 353.

Chapter 3, p. 33
Victor Hugo, *Les Misérables/Translated and with an Intro-duction by Norman Denny* (London: The Folio Society Limited, 1976), p. 1210.

Chapter 3, p. 35
Jim Elliot, *The Journals of Jim Elliot/edited by Elisabeth Elliot* (Old Tappan, NJ: F. H. Revell Co., 1978).

Chapter 3, p. 35
William H. Murray, *The Scottish Himalaya Expedition* (London: J. M. Dent & Sons Ltd., 1951), p. 7.

Chapter 3, p. 35 (Goethe quote)
Goethe's Faust/From the German by John Auster (New York: Dodd, Mead & Co., 1894), p. 28.

Chapter 5, p. 50 (Merton quote)
Thomas Merton, *No Man Is an Island* (New York: Harcourt, Brace and Company, 1955), p. 31.

Chapter 5, p. 66 (da Vinci)
Harrison Kinney, *The Last Supper of Leonardo da Vinci: An Account of Its Recreation by Lumen Martin Winter* (New York: Coward-McCann, 1953), pp. 77-78.

Chapter 7, p. 89 (William Inge quote)
Reader's Digest (New York: Reader's Digest Association, 1932), p. 108.

Chapter 7, p. 89 (Henry Ward Beecher quote)
Eleanor Kirk, *Beecher as a Humorist* (New York: Fords, Howard and Halbert, 1987), p. 81.

Chapter 9, p. 123 (Dante quote)
Dante Alighieri, *The Divine Comedy* (Chicago: Regnery Gateway, 1980), p. 362.

Chapter 9, p. 123 (Underhill quote)
Charles Wilson, *The Letters of Evelyn Underhill/Edited with an Introduction* (Westminster, MD: Christian Classics, 1989), p. 204.

Chapter 9, p. 124 (Latimer quote)
Frank Spencer Mead, *The Encyclopedia of Religious Quotations* (Westwood, NJ: Fleming H. Revell Company, 1965), p. 197.

Chapter 10, p. 132 (William Carey Quote)
Timothy George, *Faithful Witness: the Life and Mission of William Carey* (Birmingham, AL: New Hope Publications, 1991), p. 32.

Chapter 11, p. 148
Søren Kierkegaard, *Purity of Heart Is to Will One Thing; Spiritual Preparation for the Feast of Confession/Translated from the Danish, with an introductory essay by Douglas V. Steeres* (New York: Harper and Brothers, 1938).

Other Books
by Lloyd John Ogilvie

Conversation with God

In *Conversation with God,* Dr. Lloyd John Ogilvie offers a fresh approach to prayer. Prayer, like good conversation, is a matter of *listening* as well as speaking. With a passion equaled by few others, Dr. Ogilvie clearly and simply explains the many dimensions of prayer and provides a 30-day guide to encourage you to make conversation with God a part of your daily life.

God's Best for My Life

God's Best for My Life has 365 profoundly personal devotions that invite you to discover, explore, and enjoy the immeasurable blessing and love that await you when you seek Him each and every day.

Quiet Moments with God

Do you need quiet moments with the Father? Do you long for His wisdom as you face daily decisions and challenges? Satisfy your heart's desire and open yourself in His presence, learning to humbly trust and follow His gracious leading.